DO YOU NEED A

Doctor, Therapist or Guru?

Wasyl Nimenko

Goalpath Books

Published by Goalpath Books 2024

Do you need a Doctor, Therapist or Guru?

Previously published 2023 by Goalpath books as 'Doctor, Therapist of Guru?' and also as 'Carl Jung Doctor, Therapist of Guru?'

ISBN 978-1-908142-99-3

Wasyl Nimenko was born in Ipswich, England. His mother was from Tubbercurry in the west of Ireland, his father from Dnipropetrovsk (now Dnipro) in central Ukraine. After studying medicine in London from 1974-1979, he began training and working as a psychiatrist. He worked at the 2,200 bed St Bernard's Hospital *(previously known as the 'Hanwell Insane Asylum' and the 'Hanwell Pauper and Lunatic Asylum')* but left psychiatry because of the overemphasis on the chemical causes and treatments of mental health problems.

He left psychiatry to train as a GP and a psychotherapist. From 1982 - 1991 he worked with survivors of torture. He worked independently, in the NHS, with the homeless and also with the emergency services and the armed forces.

In 1984 Wasyl Nimenko researched the stress of using virtual reality for Xerox among the first users of the Xerox Star, technology which has since become the standard in personal computers. In 2011 he carried out research into the use of archaeology in the psychological decompression of wounded soldiers, a service which is now available internationally to the armed forces as 'Operation Nightingale.' In 2013 he researched Post Repatriation Stress Disorder which was first described in 2015.

Although Wasyl Nimenko's professional activities have chiefly been in the UK he has also lived and worked in India, New Zealand and Australia. At present his main interest is in uncovering, recognising and realising our natural happiness.

CONTENTS

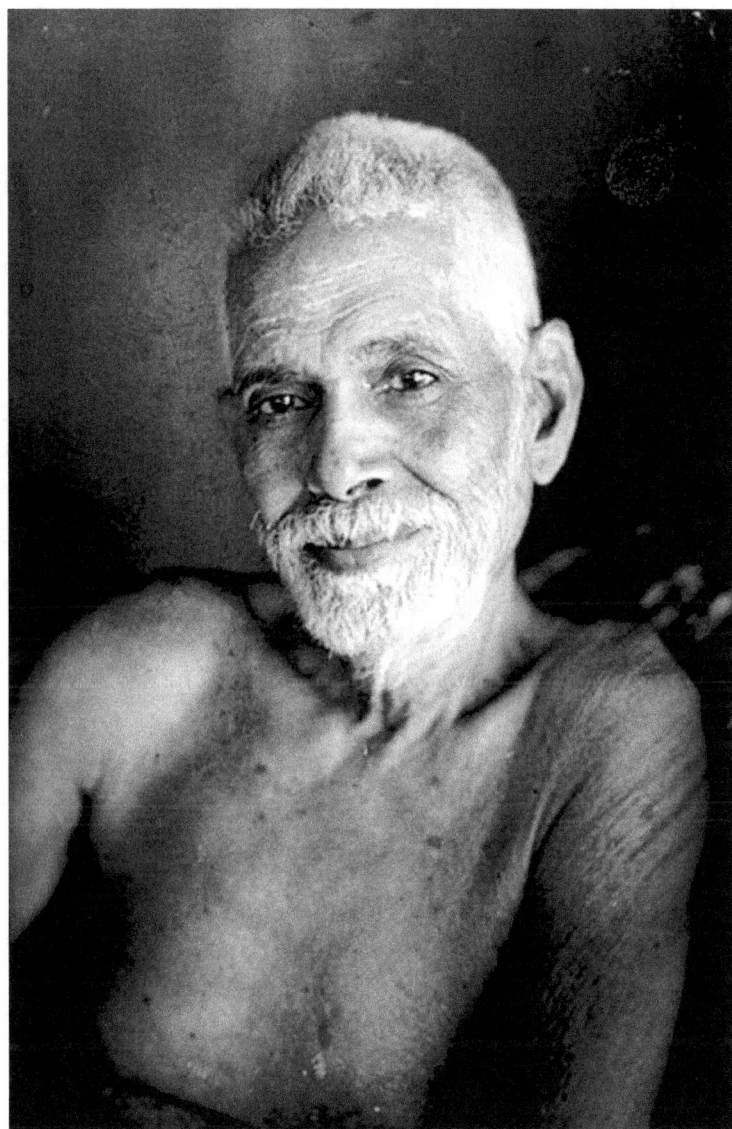

INTRODUCTION

Deciding whether to seek help from a doctor, therapist or guru is not always a clear-cut and simple task. In spite of their different spheres of activity, the three categories are not mutually exclusive. What each category has to offer is examined, including the overlapping interests in which they appear to compete.

In making a decision concerning whom to choose, it is helpful to try and gage the level of happiness of a doctor, therapist or guru. The happiness factor is at least as important as the other vital qualities of compassion, empathy and integrity. The difficulty of judging if they are "wounded healers" who are sufficiently aware of their own wounds to be helpful to others is also examined, as is the potential harm they can do.

By way of illustration, examples have been drawn from amongst the most flawed and least flawed doctors, therapists and gurus.

Throughout the enquiries conducted in this book, Carl Jung figures as an important point of reference.

The present work is written from the author's professional perspective as a doctor and psychotherapist. But it also includes a strong autobiographical element in which the author recounts his intimate personal experience of seeking a path in the pursuit of Inner Happiness.

1.

The Avoidance of Pain
and
The Path towards Happiness

1.

The Avoidance of Pain and
The Path towards Happiness

'Happiness is a matter of perspective'

When we are unhappy and want help we usually go to a doctor or a therapist. However, some people who go to see a doctor or a therapist might be better served by a guru and of course vice versa.

Looking at our search for happiness it seems like there are genuine areas of crossover of things we might want from each of these helpers at different times because what they offer is different. However, the boundaries of what they offer can overlap each other's field of work which may make things look more complicated and confusing than they are.

Understanding their differences and similarities might help choosing which one to go to.

So just why do some of us go to a guru, some to a doctor and others to a therapist when we are unhappy? Is it just a cultural difference between East and West? Or are there other influences? To understand this in depth we need to see the reasons why we go to them.

Doctors, therapists and gurus are usually but not always approached by someone who has suffered and continues carrying pain and suffering inside. We ask for help because despite trying to find a solution we remain unhappy.

To understand how differently unhappiness is viewed by doctors, therapists and gurus in their different fields of work, we need to look at the nature and causes of unhappiness and we may need to reconsider who is the best person to consult.

It has become almost automatic to medicalise and pathologise unhappiness by diagnosing and labelling types of unhappiness as diseases that are diagnosed and best treated by doctors. If we blindly accept a doctor's authority, we are at high risk of becoming passive compliant bystanders and giving up our autonomy, which in some cases could have contributed to the unhappiness in the first place.

However, if we do not blindly accept medical authority, we can open up many other possibilities to recover and restore our happiness, which is what we will be doing from here onwards.

The value of help with our physical problems from doctors is not in question but from here we will not be using any mental health terms which define diseases and designate doctors as the primary authority in understanding and curing unhappiness (mental health problems). Instead, we will simply look at unhappiness and our search for happiness.

First, 'timing' can indicate the nature of unhappiness. Although we may be unhappy about the future, our unhappiness about our past or our current circumstances are the main reasons we go to see a doctor, therapist or guru.

The most common causes of unhappiness we look for help with are neglect, emotional, physical or sexual abuse, death of a loved one or trauma as a child or adult, many of which are connected with having an alcoholic or dysfunctional parent. These usually leave us wounded with psychological scars which do not heal so easily without help. [1]

Second, 'we may not know' the nature of our unhappiness. Despite being materially secure and personally successful in our activities in the outer world, unhappiness of 'unknown origin' can also lead us to see a doctor, therapist or guru.

Third, our 'mundane existence' may seem like the only cause of our unhappiness. Some of us want to be awakened out of the misery of what seems like mundane existence to the truth of our existence. We have an intuitive sense there is more to our mundane lives and we want to know what it is.

We may even have had a brief glimpse of a direct experience of consciousness of oneness with everything. Not being able to repeat this can leave us chronically frustrated or miserable because we cannot find an answer, and this can also lead us to approach a guru.

2.

What a Therapist Offers

'A bad attitude is like a flat tyre

Until it is changed you can't go anywhere'

Unknown

2.

What a Therapist Offers

'Our thoughts can be changed by changing our attitudes'

Therapy is the formalisation of ancient wisdom with words and is as old as storytelling, as is shown by one of the most famous stories in Buddhism of Kisa Gotami's healing after the death of her young son in the time of the Buddha around 500 BCE.

'During Buddha's time, there lived a woman named Kisa Gotami. She married young and gave birth to a son. One day, the baby fell sick and died soon after. Kisa Gotami loved her son greatly and refused to believe that her son was dead. She carried the body of her son around her village, asking if there was anyone who could bring her son back to life. The villagers all saw that the son was already dead and there was nothing that could be done. They advised her to accept his death and make arrangements for the funeral. In great grief, she fell upon her knees and clutched her son's body close to her body. She kept uttering for her son to wake up. A village elder took pity on her and suggested to her to consult the Buddha. "Kisa Gotami. We cannot help you. But you should go to the Buddha. Maybe he can bring your son back to life!"

Kisa Gotami was extremely excited upon hearing the elder's words. She immediately went to the Buddha's residence and pleaded for him to bring her son back to life. "Kisa Gotami, I have a way to bring your son back to life." "My Lord, I will do anything to bring my son back" "If that is the case, then I need you to find me something. Bring me a mustard seed but it must be taken from a house where no one residing in the house has ever lost a family member. Bring this seed back to me and your son will come back to life."

Having great faith in the Buddha's promise, Kisa Gotami went from house to house, trying to find the mustard seed. At the first house, a young woman offered to give her some mustard seeds. But when Kisa Gotami asked if she had ever lost a family member to death, the young women said her grandmother died a few months ago. Kisa Gotami thanked the young woman and explained why the mustard seeds did not fulfil the Buddha's requirements. She moved on to the second house. A husband died a few years. The third house lost an uncle and the fourth house lost an aunt. She kept moving from house to house but the answer was all the same – every house had lost a family member to death. Kisa Gotami finally came to realise that there is no one in the world who had never lost a family member to death. She now understood that death is inevitable and a natural part of life. Putting aside her grief, she buried her son in the forest. She then returned to the Buddha and became his follower. '[1]

Perhaps listening to people from many households about death and loss let her see that although we experience loss uniquely, we are the same, as our loss is similar to everyone else's loss.

The Four Big Waves of Therapy

To understand therapy, we need to understand the four waves of psychology on which it is all based. *The first wave* was 'Psychoanalysis' first developed by Sigmund Freud, who has been largely discredited [2] and later by Carl Jung, also largely discredited, who formulated most of his theory whilst suffering from a long psychotic illness that lasted years. [3] Both however made valuable contributions to psychology.

The second wave of Psychologists were 'Behaviourists' who tried to understand our minds only by our behaviour. In trying to understand ourselves by getting rid of God, psychiatrists and psychologists perhaps threw out the very essence of what we see ourselves to be.

The third wave of 'Humanistic Psychology' was the response to the limitations of Psychoanalysis and Behavioural Psychology, largely by Carl Rogers and Abraham Maslow. This was based on man's drive to self-actualisation, the process of realising our own capabilities.

The fourth wave, 'Transpersonal Psychology,' includes and complements the first three and is based on the need to include the spiritual in all its many forms. It is largely due to Roberto Assagioli's work in Psychosynthesis and Abraham Maslow's work, together with the earlier work of Carl Jung and Viktor Frankl. This movement sprang up in 1969 and was not surprisingly just after the summer of love in 1967 with its challenge to traditional authority. Ian Gordon-Brown and Barbara Somers gave an account of Transpersonal Psychology in *'The Raincloud of Unknowable things.'* An important influence in that direction was from the Beatles' promotion of meditation in 1967. George Harrison played a particularly sincere and important role in this.

Transpersonal psychology integrates modern psychology with the ancient wisdom of Vedanta, Judaism, Buddhism, Christian Mysticism, Sufism meditation, alchemy and various forms of divination.

The Vital Importance of Meaning

The importance of meaning in our life is vital. As we will see later, for some people 'meaning' can eventually be realised as experiencing being conscious of 'I AM that I AM.' However, one size does not fit all.

After suffering and surviving the worst kind of trauma, such as torture or childhood sexual abuse, the single most important quality of a therapist can be the ability to re-establish a person's trust in humanity by trusting another human being.

Continually focusing and prioritising a person's needs is always vital as it highlights 'meaning' in their life. A good therapist will speak up and mention if the person needs a job or somewhere to live or a relationship more than they need therapy.

Victor Frankl observed many times that the ones who survived the Holocaust of the German concentration camps were the ones who could find meaning. He supported Nietzsche's words:

'He who has a why to live can bear with almost any how.' [4]

In our unhappiness, finding meaning can be the pivotal point of survival and recovery because having meaning

9

protects us and our health both physically and mentally.

It is deemed unlikely that someone will commit suicide if they have 'protective' factors in their life, such as close family or a project they need to finish. There needs to be meaning in their lives. [5] Therapists frequently work with suicidal people to help them recognise, emphasise or even establish protective factors in their life which can make the difference between them having temporary suicidal ideas and actually committing suicide.

Ignorance of Not Seeing Breakdown as Transformation

In Japan there is an art form of repairing broken pottery called Kintsugi. [6] The areas of breakage are repaired with glue mixed with gold dust, silver dust or platinum dust, so all the breaks are more visible. The gold cracks show that when repaired with all its scars visible, the imperfect piece of pottery may be more beautiful than the original. It represents the acceptance of transience and imperfection in keeping with the Japanese world view of 'Wabi-sabi' [7] and also the philosophy of 'Mushin,' [8] in that the damage is not hidden but illuminated, to represent equanimity and detachment amid changing conditions. Kintsugi can also represent a restorative process of a better changed perspective, of healing and wholeness.

The most in-depth account of this is given by an experienced psychotherapist Elizabeth Wilde McCormick in 'Living on the Edge: Breaking up to Breakdown to Breakthrough,' where she draws on medical and psychological theory, anthropology, religious and spiritual tradition, art and poetry to look at the edge and the prospect of the hidden gifts it can bring. [9]

In Transpersonal Psychotherapy [10] wisdom from various forms of divination like the I Ching, Astrology or Tarot cards can sometimes be helpful in therapy. The most important card in the Tarot card deck of 78 cards is 'The Fool,' which in the 15th Century meant madman or beggar. The Fool represents our quest for truth to see our true Self. The Fool has simple faith in the Universe and is unaware of the hardships and pain they will experience on their journey. During their journey, the fool is taken through the great mysteries of life, becomes aware of their ignorance, sheds their ego and is transformed by finding happiness inside. [11] This can help normalise a difficult time in our life.

Astrology is concerned with the effects of celestial mechanics on terrestrial events and is based on the principle of 'as above so below,' which originated from the Hermetic tradition around 200 BCE. This may have been influenced by Anaximander's 600 BCE earlier concept of the Multiverse. The Multiverse includes all space, all of time, all matter, and energy, the planets, stars and galaxies, other parallel Universes, all consciousness, and everything known and unknown. [12]

The Multiverse was an early record like the concept of Brahman or consciousness of the eternal, or I AM That I AM. It can also be a convenient way of agnostics and atheists having some sense of everything, the Cosmic Self without using the word God, which can be helpful in therapy. The I-Ching can also help someone surrender their sense of ego and to be more conscious of fate rather than the apparent control by their will. [13]

Therapists perform a particularly difficult task and do it with good results but it is estimated that approximately 3-10% of patients become worse after psychotherapy, with higher rates of 7-15% for patients with 'substance abuse.' [14]

The most easily available talking therapies [15] and free 'online' therapies are Artificial Intelligence (AI) based interactive algorithms, without any other human involved. Of course, this may suit some people.

At the other end of the scale of therapies, one of the most effective ones, specifically for psychological trauma, regarded as the gold standard is 'Eye Movement Desensitisation and Reprogramming' (EMDR). [16]

There are also many different types of specialist support groups and dozens of types of talking therapies available including art therapy, music therapy and drama therapy, child therapy and couples therapy to mention only a few.

Mutual Aid - Perhaps the Most Effective Help

Much of the help for most of our unhappiness should be demonetised, de-medicalised, de-therapised and then mutualised in 'mutual aid' support groups. Mutual Aid was first thought of by Peter Kropotkin around 1900.

Mutual aid groups are specific support groups which can be more appropriate and more effective than seeing a therapist, although a therapist can also be helpful. These groups are free of charge, are available worldwide. They are regarded by many as the most effective form of receiving help and support from people who are experienced and have got better by participating in these groups.

These experienced people who have succeeded in dealing with their problem are regarded by many doctors and therapists as the 'real' experts as opposed to professional medical experts who may have no personal experience of these special problems. Some of the successful members of these groups often go on to become professional experts in the medical industry. However, both they and their clients almost always end up using the free voluntary services provided by these groups as they are not monetised help and therefore seem more authentic and more acceptable.

For example, Al-Anon the mutual aid support group for family members of alcoholics or anyone affected by someone else's drinking [17] provides an anonymous forum to share with others their experience, strength and hope. For many, this may be their most important source of help, just as Alcoholics Anonymous (AA) is for alcoholics [18], [19] where 24% remain sober after 5 years [20] and for many no other therapy may be necessary.

Similar support groups exist for others specific problems such as people with eating disorders in Eating Disorders Anonymous (EDA). [21] Eating disorders are the most lethal of mental illnesses with the highest mortality rate. There are also groups for those with sex addiction in Sex Addiction Anonymous (SAA) [22] and those addicted to gambling in Gamblers Anonymous (GA). [23] There are also free mutual aid support groups for people addicted to drugs such as cocaine in Narcotics Anonymous (NA) [24] and those addicted to cannabis in Marijuana Anonymous (MA). [25]

13

3.

What Doctors Offer

'The only authority on happiness is your Self'

3.

What Doctors Offer

'Medicalising happiness results in more unhappiness'

In June 2022, the World Health Organisation (WHO) stated that 1 in every 8 people in the world live with a mental disorder, with Depression and Anxiety being the most common. [1] That is around one billion people.

As mentioned, the most common causes of unhappiness we look for help with are neglect, emotional, physical or sexual abuse as a child, death of a loved one or trauma as a child or adult, many of which are connected with having an alcoholic or dysfunctional parent. These difficulties usually leave us wounded with psychological scars which do not easily go away without help.

We tend to go to a doctor first with most problems, simply because all sorts of symptoms even tiredness, a low mood or not coping can be a sign of an underlying disease and we want to know and be reassured that there is no physical disease causing our unhappiness. Simple tests can reassure the doctor and ourselves that the cause is not physical.

Most doctors still medicalise our unhappiness and treat us with medication but some suggest we see a therapist. This indicates some doctors accept that unhappiness is not due to a chemical imbalance and making us happy is beyond their field of knowledge, expertise or interests. This takes our unhappiness out of their field of competence. However, we may still choose another easy option of a 'quick fix' solution to our unhappiness by self-medicating with alcohol or other drugs which 10% of us do at some time to the point of addiction. [2]

Thought Control by Sedation is Not Scientific

As we have seen, thinking is the single common denominator that makes us unhappy about anything. However, GPs, Psychiatrists and mental health workers use the antidepressant class of 'Selective Serotonin Uptake Inhibitors' (SSRIs) to increase Serotonin levels in the brain. They do this because they still accept the 'Serotonin Theory' put forward in the 1960s (but never proved) that depression is due to low Serotonin levels in the brain.

These drugs, with varying degrees of severity, change many people into virtual cabbages in that the peaks and the troughs of their feelings are gone. Consciousness is reduced and their emotions are numbed. In other words, the lowest points of unhappiness are gone but so is their ability to experience peaks of happiness. They are therefore of course more easily controlled socially and medically. But inside they often describe themselves as 'half awake, half asleep, numb, sedated and half dead.' It can be extremely difficult to stop taking these drugs because of withdrawal effects. So once on them, they are already hooked.

Although doctors perform their duties diligently and professionally and manage to improve the physical and mental health of most of their patients, it should be noted that 6% of patients are exposed to preventable harm while in medical care. [3]

In the July 2022 issue of the journal 'Nature' there was a systematic umbrella review of the evidence for the serotonin theory of depression. [4] SSRIs are the most commonly used medication worldwide for anxiety and depression and include Citalopram, Escitalopram, Fluoxetine, Paroxetine and Sertraline. Umbrella reviews are regarded as one of the highest levels of evidence currently used in medicine. The conclusion of the researchers was:

"This review suggests that the huge research effort based on the serotonin hypothesis has not produced convincing evidence of a biochemical basis to depression. This is consistent with research on many other biological markers. We suggest it is time to acknowledge that the serotonin theory of depression is not empirically substantiated."

Basically, since 1987, the pharmaceutical industry (Big Pharma) got away with hoodwinking the world into believing they had specific pharmaceutical cures for depression. This article has been welcomed by many but not all doctors as it presents an irrefutable challenge to Big Pharma and the beginning of a long-awaited move away from medication to therapy. Despite this, in November 2022 Big Pharma was still encouraging people to use these antidepressants and continued to publish studies without any convincing evidence of the serotonin theory. [5] Maybe we have to accept there will always be 'Snake oil' salesmen.

If we hear and listen to this long overdue 'barn door' evidence in communication from some of the world's most respected scientists, we cannot say anything other than it is time to de-medicalise and remove unhappiness from the field of competence of the medical profession.

Many doctors have known this for decades but have been unwilling to make a stand against the uselessness of medication for our unhappiness because they are caught up in the complicated web of being funded by the establishment which is in the pocket of Big Pharma.

Up until the beginning of the twentieth century help for problems with our happiness came under the authority of religious priests and other healers. As the popularity of religions continued to drop dramatically, their role of officiating at births, deaths, marriages and funerals became simply functional like the services provided by airline staff on routine flights. Doctors reassured by Big Pharma took up the challenge of looking after and medicalising our unhappiness.

We have to unlearn almost a century of being misguided by doctors and accept that unhappiness is not due to altered brain chemicals but is part of the human condition of living. When we accept this, we have to turn elsewhere and the first option is therapy, which can come in many forms.

Social Prescribing as Trivialising Unhappiness

'Social prescribing' is the referral of patients to support services in the community. It can include activities such as gardening, singing classes and many other activities. It has been taken up because it is seen by some as having the advantage of reducing the cost of healthcare. It has been practiced worldwide for a long time and has recently been formalised and promoted.

Its recent growth is most likely an attempt to ease the strain on doctors in pressurised healthcare systems of large numbers of unhappy patients. Social prescribing was designed to help medical patients who are lonely, isolated or have complex medical needs. Social prescribing reflects the inability of doctors to directly help people's unhappiness. It shows some indication that doctors do not believe that medical drugs are always the best answer for unhappiness.

Despite a British Medical Journal systematic review of evidence from 15 research evaluations, studies failed to provide any good evidence that 'social prescribing' is successful. [6] But social prescribing is still being widely promoted and adopted by just over half of UK GPs. [7]

This is probably an expression of frustration of some doctors that they are stuck with being the authority on unhappiness even though they lack the knowledge and skills to help people become less unhappy. The lack of uptake by more GPs and patients could be because social prescribing may be seen as trivialising our unhappiness when it is already downgraded by doctors who are more concerned with physical health problems.

Healing Influences Without Doctors or Therapists

Evidence showing that going to a guru can help us has been seen in research from South India. In 2002 the Internationally respected 'British Medical Journal' reported important medical research findings from The Muthuswamy Temple in Tamil Nadu in South India. [8]

The Muthuswamy Temple was built in a graveyard, over the tomb of Muthuswamy, a man who lived in the village a century ago. Muthuswamy spent his time wandering about the village, probably as a mendicant. Villagers noticed that a mere touch of his hand cured many ailments, especially mental illnesses. Muthuswamy had died many years before, but his influence on people's mental health was believed to be present as if he was still living.

Thirty-one individuals with a wide range of severe psychiatric illnesses briefly stayed in the Muthuswamy Temple and were rated on standard psychiatric rating scales before and after their stay. There was no charge for their average stay of six weeks and they were in a supportive non-threatening environment with no healing rituals. The research results indicated that a short stay in this temple equalled the therapeutic benefits of standard modern psychiatric treatment.

When such good results were obtained in people with a wide range of severe mental health problems, we can only imagine the possible benefits for others with less severe problems. Individuals who go to the Muthuswamy Temple do not go there because of promotion of research findings; they go there because of attraction, usually by word of mouth, the same way most people find their guru.

This brings us back to our inner silent stillness which is experienced by many who visit sites where a sage or a guru's remains are present. Such visits can obviously provide rest and peace away from the stress and strain of our ordinary lives and could mistakenly be seen as a holiday but they provide so much more than just an escape from everyday life. They probably provide many of the benefits of what are known as pilgrimages. They may have added benefits, perhaps because of the length of stay enabling a person to 'stabilise' in a non-threatening, non-judgemental environment.

Visits to places like this are not just a retreat from life to a sanctuary but are an opportunity to turn inwards. Sometimes turning inwards can be difficult, even distressing at first so in such places, silence, inactivity and detachment from the outer world are encouraged in favour of the inner world. The current medical approach could scarcely differ more.

Medical Treatment in Hospital

The current medical approach has changed little since 1982-1983 when I was training as a psychiatrist working on acute psychiatric wards in London at the 2,200 bed St Bernard's Hospital, which was previously known as the 'Hanwell Insane Asylum' and the 'Hanwell Pauper and Lunatic Asylum.' As it was then, it is still standard practice in almost all acute psychiatric hospitals for nursing staff to physically restrain patients and forcibly give them injections of powerful tranquilisers to control their behaviour.

Almost all psychiatrists admit they do not understand the cause or cure of serious mental health problems such as psychosis or severe depression. In these conditions, almost all psychiatrists admit that they are usually using the same drugs they were using fifty years ago, which are basically cousins of the original drugs, mainly differing in having less severe side effects. Almost all psychiatrists admit that they do not understand how these drugs work or indeed why in many cases they do not work.

During the acute stages of severe of mental illnesses psychiatrists see their primary function as providing safe and secure surroundings in a psychiatric hospital for individuals who are a danger to themselves and to others. This frequently involves physical restraint and forcible administration of powerful tranquilisers. Whilst doing this various medications are tried in an often vain attempt to cure.

It seems logical that physically restraining patients by psychiatric nursing staff and forcibly giving them injections of powerful tranquilisers to control their behaviour is good humane medical care. This is done in the belief that this makes it easier and quicker to contain patients on a ward and until their behaviour shows that they are no longer a danger to themselves and others. This of course seems the logical rational thing to do in the interests of safety until it is compared with the methods used at the Muthuswamy Temple where results are the same.

One study found that whilst being treated in a psychiatric hospital, 31% of patients experienced physical assault, 8% experienced sexual assault, 63% reported witnessing traumatic events and 54% experienced potentially harmful experiences, such as being around frightening or violent patients.

These are very frequent and severe side effects of psychiatric in-patient treatment which often appear as Post Traumatic Stress Disorder (PTSD), one of the most common symptoms of which is avoidant behaviour. Because of this, after leaving hospital many patients avoid using mental health services in the future and forfeit the support which this could provide.[9]

The traumatic effects of being in a 'Straight Jacket' have not gone. Treatment now takes the form of 'chemical restraint.'

Although it seems that psychiatric treatment is generally helpful and appropriate, deep down we know it is not ideal, even though it is given with the best intentions and great care by nursing staff. However well intentioned, we know psychiatric treatment is frequently traumatic and may indeed cause some of the very conditions it purports to treat such as PTSD.

We only agree to go along with psychiatric treatment because it seems like the only course available. But there are equally effective alternative treatments as shown by the scientific results of the Muthuswamy Temple.

Doctors are easily taken in by the 'Snake oil' salesmen of Big Pharma and are also taken in by fellow doctors who set themselves up as authorities in psychiatry and psychology.

The introduction of psychoanalysis by Sigmund Freud and Carl Jung has 'not' altered our understanding of severe psychiatric disorders in meaningful or helpful ways. Instead, Freud and Jung demonstrated the lengths to which psychiatrists could be allowed go to set themselves up as gurus running cults explaining everything from understanding the nature of happiness to the cause and cure of serious psychiatric disorders. Sigmund Freud's and Carl Jung's deeply flawed influence as false gurus is explained in Anthony Storr's book, *Feet of Clay*.

We can only intelligently conclude that considering the

research results from the Muthuswamy Temple indicated a short stay there equalled the therapeutic benefits of standard modern psychiatric treatment, it is astonishing that similar research projects have not been replicated and rigorously tested elsewhere. [10]

We can only hope that this research happens soon and that more successful different ways are found to help those with all kinds of mental health problems.

4.

What a Guru Offers

'Being happy is the stillness of our Self'

4.

What a Guru Offers

'Ask yourself whether you are happy and you will cease to be so'

John Stuart Mill

Thinking is the single common denominator that makes us unhappy about anything. To stop negative or wrong thinking from making us unhappy, first we have to control our thinking and then we have to use this to stop our thinking to let our mind be still without thought and to see things as they are and not as we wish or expect them to be. This is happiness. Whatever way you control thoughts to stop them, sustained concentration during meditation is a fight and effortless awareness only comes after great effort. It is a process of subtraction and not addition in that we are stopping thoughts, not adding anything new.

What we want in our relationship with a Guru can be vastly different from what we want from a doctor or therapist. The principal difference in our relationship with a guru is our aim, through the stillness of having no thoughts, to have direct experience of oneness with everything.

But the reasons why we go to see a Guru may initially be the same reasons why we go to see doctors and therapists. Often, we may go to see a guru because we did not find a solution for our unhappiness with doctors or therapists.

We do not go to see a guru because we are happy. We go because we are unhappy. A brief reminder of the most common reasons for this will keep things in perspective.

Firstly, the most common causes of unhappiness we look for help with are neglect, emotional, physical or sexual abuse, death of a loved one or trauma as a child or adult. Many of these are connected with having an alcoholic or otherwise dysfunctional parent.

Secondly, 'we may not know' the nature of our unhappiness. Despite being materially secure and personally successful in our activities in the outer world, unhappiness of 'unknown origin' can also lead us to see a doctor, therapist or guru.

Thirdly, the tedium of our existence may seem like the only cause of our unhappiness. Some of us want to be awakened out of the misery of what seems like mundane existence to the truth of our existence. We have an intuitive sense there is more to our mediocre lives and we want to know what it is.

As we mentioned earlier, we may even have had a brief glimpse of a direct experience of consciousness of oneness with everything. Not being able to repeat this can leave us chronically frustrated or miserable because we cannot find an answer, and this can also lead us to approach a guru.

What we want is permanent happiness that is not affected by the vicissitudes of our daily lives or the rest of the world. We are trying to change and re-set our default from 'thinking' to 'being conscious' of the oneness of everything.'

When we see we are limited in our understanding and experience of looking inwards, we know we are stuck and need help and guidance from someone who knows the inner territory of silent stillness better than we do. This is when we go to a guru.

In choosing a guru we are best guided by the silent stillness of a one who exemplifies this quality rather than one who speaks volumes. Stillness is not found through thinking but arises from not thinking.

Silent Stillness

From all the gurus we will give special consideration to one of the least known. The sage Ramana Maharshi gained the attention and respect of Carl Jung.

Even though Jung did not meet him whilst he was in India, most of the chapter 'The Holy Men of India' in Jung's *'Collected Works'* was concerned with Ramana Maharshi:

'Sri Ramana Maharshi is a true son of the Indian Earth. He is "genuine," and on top of that he is a "phenomenon," which seen through European eyes, has claims to uniqueness. But in India he is merely the whitest spot on a white surface.' [1]

The Dalai Lama also echoed this:

'The heritage of India is enriched with numberless saints and yogis. Ramana Maharshi represents that tradition and his spiritual greatness is guiding millions of people. Such masters light the path and bring solace to suffering humanity.' [2]

The English psychiatrist Anthony Storr in his last book *Feet of Clay*, which was about Gurus with major hidden flaws, advised what is the most important quality of a guru:

"If someone must seek a guru it is best to choose one who does not speak."[3]

The written recorded dialogues over three years in the book, *Talks with Sri Ramana Maharshi* [4] show that Ramana Maharshi spoke only on 220 out of 1095 days; roughly once every 5 days which by any standard is virtual silence. As we will see in the next chapter Ramana Maharshi's silent stillness was able to console a woman who seemed inconsolable after the death of her husband [5].

Ramana Maharshi is not well known because there is no promotion or advertising of him. His teaching was mainly through silent stillness. There is no recording of his voice. He did not indicate a successor to teach his way or impart his wisdom. There are no teachers or courses. Today he is found by almost gravitational attraction, for example by a chance coming across a photograph, a mention in a book or a mention of his name.

Escaping from the Misery of Mundane Life

Although he is a unique phenomenon, his life follows the pattern of other spiritual teachers His early life was not without suffering. When he was twelve years old his father died with the result that his family was broken up and he moved to Dindigul with his mother and then Madurai to

31

live with his uncle.

At twelve years old he experienced the pain of losing his father, seeing his mother's grief, the upheaval of leaving his parental home, leaving his school and his friends as well as having to move in with an uncle. This would have been an abrupt end to an otherwise happy childhood with his parents, siblings and friends. He hints at being rescued from the pain of the misery of life in a verse:

'To rescue me - born of virtuous Sundara and Sundari in the holy place of Tiruchuli, seat of Bhuminatheswara - from the pain of miserable mundane life, He raised me to His state, that His heart might so rejoice, the immanence of Siva so shine forth, and the Self flourish. Such is Arunachala, famous throughout the universe!' [6]

Perhaps his difficult childhood paved the way for him to have his first experience of realisation with absolute certainty of his Self which he describes as having at 16 years old. [7] Arthur Osborne stated this most clearly when he said:

'It sometimes happens that one who is on a spiritual path, or even who has not yet begun consciously seeking, has a glimpse of Realisation during which, for a brief eternity, he experiences absolute certainty of his divine, immutable, universal Self.' [8]

When he saw an opportunity of going to a spiritual centre, the hill Arunachala, which he had not previously known actually existed; he simply left his uncle's home to live on Arunachala for good. He regarded this hill Arunachala as his guru.

The Legacy of Silent Stillness

His legacy is the consciousness of the silent stillness that he emanated, and directly experiencing the happiness of this oneness ourselves. His legacy is the 'direct path,' or final common path to which all attempts at realisation must eventually come. The following is a summary of how he explained this.

He always suggested asking the question, 'Who am I?' and he also frequently stated that the Self, the Guru and also God are one and the same. So, what does this mean? It means that when we directly experience the consciousness of oneness with everything, of being one with the eternal, i.e., with the Guru and with God, we experience with absolute certainty our universal Self. This is seen by conscious intuition and is verifiable from personal experience rather than by theory or logic. It is experiential knowledge. Thus, we are awakened to the truth of our existence. This is what is meant by having our ignorance removed, to find meaning and be happy. At first, this experience may be limited to a brief glimpse.

In helping us to answer the question, 'Who am I?' Ramana Maharshi quotes the *Book of Exodus* in the Old Testament, where Moses asks the Burning Bush what to tell the Israelites the name of God is. The voice of God from the Burning bush replies saying, "I AM That I AM."

In using this quote 'I AM That I AM.' Ramana Maharshi means we must remove our false sense of who we are i.e., that we are a bundle of thoughts called the ego and become aware we are the cosmic Self, 'That' which is everything.

33

He summarised the truth and the method simply by saying:

'Your duty is to be: and not to be this or that. "I AM that I AM"[9] *sums up the whole truth. The method is summed up in "BE STILL". What does "stillness" mean? It means "destroy yourself". Because any form or shape is the cause of trouble. Give up the notion that "I am so and so." '*[10]

He saw lasting happiness is only achieved by turning inwards, away from misery when he said:

'What is happiness? Happiness is the very nature of the Self; happiness and the Self are not different. There is no happiness in any object of the world. We imagine through our ignorance that we derive happiness from objects. When the mind goes out, it experiences misery.' [11]

5.

Choosing a
Wounded Healer

'Just as true happiness only comes after suffering, only those with a healed wound can heal'

5.

Choosing a Wounded Healer

'There are no happy unflawed people'

In choosing a therapist the most important thing is your intuitive judgment on meeting them of whether they seem the right person for you. Most of the time our intuition is right but sometimes our intuition can be wrong and we may need to try more than one therapist. Being aware of our own imperfection and persevering indicates our commitment and sincerity in finding the right path.

Just like gurus and doctors, therapists can have major faults which can do us harm, so choosing one is not without risk. The risk is usually lessened by a good recommendation. Doctors, therapists often have the same negative qualities. A sure sign of such false prophets is advertising or promotion of their services. Good doctors, therapists and gurus attract people by word of mouth for their integrity and their reputation for successful outcomes. They do not need to promote themselves.

Although doctors, therapists and gurus all try to restore our happiness they inhabit different territories. We are not always the centre of their attention. The person seeking help should not be merely treated as a number in a research trial or research data to promote their careers to bring them fame or fortune.

The most helpful doctor, therapist or guru to us obviously needs to have more knowledge and experience than us but also vitally important, we need to intuitively sense a selfless concern for others along with compassion.

Unlike gurus, both therapists and doctors, have to have been formally trained and be qualified and registered with a recognised professional organisation. Therapists must be insured and have ongoing supervision throughout all the time they are practicing.

Good therapists will have personal experience of pain and suffering through which they have worked. It would be almost impossible for a good therapist to have no wounds and be squeaky clean of psychological scars. But there must be a balance in that they cannot be so damaged that it affects their listening and understanding or harms their clients. It is an unspoken acknowledgement that a therapist has to be a wounded healer to be able to heal. A good account of wounded healers is given by Claire Dunne in, Carl Jung: Wounded Healer of the Soul. [1]

We can have difficulty in deciding whether to see a doctor, therapist or a guru if we are not quite sure of the source of our unhappiness. This difficulty in choosing from a doctor therapist or guru can be further confused if it is not clear what a particular doctor, therapist or guru is offering us. Therefore, we should try and find out and also ask them what they have to give us.

A doctor can try and help us stop our thinking by using medication that sedates us so much that our thinking reduces our unhappiness and also reduces the peace of happiness. We lose the peaks and troughs of happiness and unhappiness.

A therapist can try and help us change our thinking by changing our attitudes.

A guru can help us stop our thinking and reset our default from mainly thinking to having experiences of oneness with everything, to being conscious of happiness more of the time until it is permanent.

But for some of us, going to see a doctor, a therapist or a support group, although helpful, does not necessarily put us on the path to find the happiness we are looking for. We may not trust them; we may not want to take medication, or the doctor or therapist does not seem to understand the nature of our problem. We may not be able to engage with and benefit from them because of our embarrassment, our fear, our shame, our guilt or because we just have needs they cannot help us with.

So, what do you do if you have already seen several doctors, therapists, tried various medications and practiced all their relaxation methods but you still cannot seem to find inner happiness? Here we return to the guru.

Our Wordless Self

Whilst doctors and therapists measure the results of work with tests and questionnaires to try and evaluate how our thinking is changed by their interventions of medication or therapy, similar evaluation of the effects of our relationship with a guru cannot be assessed or quantified and compared. This is because a change in our experience of consciousness is beyond words and is unmeasurable and will probably remain so.

We have seen that when we are unhappy it can be difficult to see what we need to be happy and whether we should see a doctor, a therapist or a guru. Also, because sometimes there are no words to express progress toward our goal, we can have difficulty in saying how we are in relation to what the goal is. We may find it difficult to articulate what we are actually looking for. Sometimes we may simply know being on the path is the same as the goal. The goal is the path and the path is the goal. There is no word for the path being indistinguishable from the destination.

Our Self-Surrender

During times of unhappiness, perseverance and patience can be our most valuable qualities. Trusting and accepting the care of a doctor, therapist or guru is a step to trusting, accepting and surrendering to the power we intuitively know is in us.

It is scientifically proven in medicine that without taking a genuine pill, the placebo response of our hopes and expectations from within us can be partly responsible for healing. However, the way this works is unknown and not understood by any psychological or neurological science, but we know it works. Most important we have the ability to heal and restore our happiness from inside when we actually believe help is possible. [2]

Our Self-Restorative Happiness

Returning to our understanding and consciousness of the Universe and even the Multiverse, where other unknown universes might exist, it is possible that what is inside us and also outside us are in some way connected and trying to re-establish the balance lost between what is outside us and inside us.

In the absence of any rational explanation, the mechanism by which this balance is restored might well be seen in how a woman, who seemed inconsolable after she witnessed the violent death of her husband, was healed by the silent look of stillness and compassion which she received from a guru, after having visited many wise and holy men. Katya Osborne recalls this incident perfectly in a short YouTube.

A woman from the north of India had been swimming with her husband in the sea in Madras when in front of her eyes he was taken by a shark. She couldn't cope with it. She went everywhere seeing wise men and holy men to ask, 'What did we do wrong? Who did we harm? We married each other. We behaved correctly. Why?'

She had found that many people had talked to her, but when she went out, she couldn't remember what they had said. They had used long phrases about the soul and spirituality. She wanted an answer. She visited the Osborne family in the southern town of Tiruvannamalai, whilst going to see the Indian sage Ramana Maharshi.

Katya Osborne, who was a young girl at that time recalls her experience and says that she couldn't bear sitting with the woman because she was tense and wound up. Katya was asked to take the woman to see Ramana Maharshi and she showed the woman into the Hall where Ramana Maharshi sat.

At the sound of the lunch time bell, Katya went to get her to take her back home. When she got back to the hall Katya saw the woman and still says.

'She was at peace and I couldn't believe it. I couldn't believe that this was the same women that I couldn't bear to be with a couple of hours ago. So, I wanted to ask her what he had said because I thought to myself, whatever he had said to her . . . those words must be the most important words in the World, they changed this woman completely, what are they, what did he say? I thought my mother will ask her, then I will find out. So we came home and my mother did ask her what he said and the woman answered.'

'Nothing.' She had her list of questions which she took out. When he looked at her, he looked so compassionate, she suddenly thought, 'It doesn't matter.' She left the list of questions and came out of the hall.

The silent look of compassion this woman received had such a profound effect on her that its impact was not only seen and felt by Katya when she collected her and can be seen today when she tells her story to share with others on You Tube. [3]

Perhaps the mechanism of this inner restorative power is triggered inside us by a guru outside of us, a therapist or even by a passing comment or a glance from someone. We do not know.

Brief Glimpse of Oneness

If this mechanism of connection occurs, then it could

42

help explain the statement that the Self, Guru and the Multiverse/God are one and the same as our consciousness of oneness with everything, that is, being conscious of true happiness.

Although words may be inadequate to describe a brief glimpse of experiencing oneness with everything, that is, being conscious of happiness, once we have this experience, we know with certainty it is what we want.

We also know what we do not want and perhaps this certainty helps us discriminate between the skills of doctors, therapists and gurus and their varying degrees of knowledge and wisdom. Seeing their functions more clearly helps us to choose who can help us.

Grace or Charisma

Last, a word of caution. There is a quality we have not mentioned and we should not overlook. We have not looked at something more usually referred to as a quality present in some gurus known as grace. Being in the presence of an authentic person with grace is entirely different from being in the presence of someone with charisma.

Someone with charisma may be confident and charming but they usually broadcast more about their external personality than inner stillness and compassion, which may be completely lacking. Stillness sits uncomfortably with charisma as they are usually incompatible.

Recognising a charismatic person can be difficult and requires good judgement. When we are looking for help, we are often at our most vulnerable and cannot easily access our discernment but eventually we find our way back to be on our own path which is itself an accomplishment as well as the goal. [4]

I would caution any involvement with charismatic individuals who set themselves up as gurus because they often do so for financial gain.

When we escape from being taken in by a charismatic personality, if we persevere, a guru can help us on the path to stop our thinking. They can reset our default from mainly thinking and having brief glances of oneness with everything, to being conscious of happiness more of the time until this consciousness becomes permanent.

Perhaps the force at work inside us is best described by Ramana Maharshi:

'The Guru is both exterior and interior. From the exterior he gives a push to the mind to turn inward; from the interior he pulls the mind towards the Self and helps the mind to achieve quietness. That is Grace. Hence there is no difference between God, Guru and Self.' [5]

6.

Inner Stillness
versus
Outer Intellect

'The path and the goal are the same'

6.

Inner Stillness
versus
Outer Intellect

'When you point a finger there are three fingers pointing back at you'

Unknown

In late autumn 1937, Carl Jung travelled to India at the invitation of the British government to attend celebrations of the University of Calcutta, where he would be awarded an honorary degree. Earlier in the same year he had received two visitors from India: V. Subramanya Iyer, spiritual advisor to the Maharajah of Mysuru, and his student Paul Brunton, the author of *'A Search in Secret India.'* [1] This meeting may have stimulated Jung's desire to visit this ancient land of wisdom. (See Appendix One)

Jung had become aware of Ramana Maharshi through his friend, the great Indologist Heinrich Zimmer who wrote a book *The Way to the Self* [2] in which Ramana Maharshi figured prominently. It is likely that Jung considered the idea that he should meet Ramana Maharshi who was reputed to be a genuine holy man who transcended the limitations of identification with the body and mind and was immersed in 'the Self.'

Jung sailed from Marseilles and landed in Bombay. He visited Delhi, the Taj Mahal, Sanchi, Allahabad, Varanasi and then onto Calcutta. The Himalayas near Darjeeling impressed him deeply. He also visited the sacred sun temple at Konark in Odisha. He was hospitalised for ten days in Calcutta after a bout of dysentery and after recovery, sailed to Madras and thence on to Colombo where he explored the Buddhist temple of Kandy and nearby Buddhist ruins. After a stay in Thiruvananthapuram, he returned to Europe.

The journey stimulated his ground-breaking study of alchemy that he had been struggling with for years. He began to make sense of the arcane language the alchemists employed bearing on the creation, not of material gold but the soul. He became so absorbed in his alchemical studies that he never left the ship at Bombay on the return leg.

During his travels in India Jung could not but be aware of Ramana Maharshi, particularly during his stay in nearby Madras. And he could not avoid making a decision whether to see Ramana Maharshi even if it meant deliberately not addressing the opportunity. Jung had borrowed his fundamental idea of 'the Self' from the East and in particular the Upanishads, of which Ramana Maharshi was a considered a living exemplar.

Jung was at the time one of the world's most influential psychiatrists. He was also a pioneer in bringing the wisdom of the East to Europe. The engagement of the West with Eastern philosophy and mysticism which he proposed is influential even today.

Jung's comments about Ramana Maharshi can probably be best understood by reflecting on the origins of his mental state. An understanding of this sheds new light on why he did not visit Tiruvannamalai. We will then see that the actual reason for Jung not visiting is quite different from the reasons he gave at the time.

In the chapter, 'The Holy Men of India,' Jung gave an unclear and confusing picture of why he didn't visit Tiruvannamalai, which also contains a degree of ambivalence. [3]
(See: https://carljungdepthpsychologysite.blog/2022/10/29/ramana-maharshi/)

It seems that Jung was more than just hesitant. If we learn more about the people who knew Jung and his own later writing this should enable us to penetrate Jung's defences and reveal the truth about why he deliberately avoided Ramana Maharshi. He then attempted to conceal the real reasons for doing this.

Jung a psychiatrist himself and a man of extraordinarily erudition suffered from prolonged mental illness. At first it seems difficult to understand him but this is really only because he deliberately concealed so very much about himself in both the chapter 'The Holy Men of India' and in his autobiography. However, Jung left a trail of evidence in his subsequent correspondence. Trying to understand Jung is rather like trying to understand a never seen before multifaceted object like a car. The only way to assess it is to slowly walk around it so that you see a different view through each facet. Perhaps this careful but circumspect approach will enable us to not to be dismissive of Jung but understand him and his legacy and why he behaved the way he did.

Jung's early childhood experiences had a profound effect on him. He came from a deeply religious family. His mother was the daughter of a theologian and his father

49

was a pastor. Two of his paternal uncles and eight of his maternal uncles were ministers in the Protestant church. But Jung's family environment was very troubled and his mother had serious and enduring mental health problems. Today the child Jung would be on the 'at risk' register for children.' [4]

Jung's mother had a nervous breakdown when he was three years old which resulted in a long separation while she recovered in hospital. Later, he suffered a series of anxiety dreams whose terrors would frequently wake him in the night. He also described visual hallucinations similar to those experienced by schizophrenics in a psychotic episode. [5]

When he was a young boy, he had already begun rebelling against Christianity. In his autobiography Jung described an important fantasy.

'I saw before me the cathedral, the blue sky. God sits on His golden throne, high above the world—and from under the throne an enormous turd falls upon the sparkling new roof, shatters it, and breaks the walls of the cathedral asunder.'

This seems to be the first evidence of him rejecting Christianity. [6] This rejection of Christianity is also the rejection of a male figure who Jung looked up to. But this was to happen twice more. In one of his letters to Freud, Jung admitted that he was traumatised as a young boy by a middle aged close friend of the family whom he looked up to. [7]

Freud neither acknowledged this surprising sensitively written confession, nor validated Jung's trauma, which might have been the first step in healing Jung's area of obvious distress. Freud demonstrated an appalling lack of compassion. Jung's reaction is unknown but knowing how sensitive and susceptible he was he would probably have been both outraged and massively disappointed. Perhaps Jung began to see that Freud, like his father and the trusted abuser, was flawed.

Jung had looked up to Freud as a father figure with almost like a god-like qualities. His acrimonious split with Freud after their last meeting on 8th September 1913 resulted in a four year period 1914-1918 of mental illness which he describes as a psychotic breakdown.

During his illness Jung had a vision where he saw an enormous flood consisting of blood and thousands of bodies. He interpreted this as being not a psychotic episode but as a prophetic premonition of the Great War.

"Towards the autumn of 1913, the pressure which I had felt was in me seemed to be moving outwards, as though there was something in the air . . . I realised that a frightful catastrophe was in progress. I saw the mighty yellow waves, the floating rube of civilisation, and the drowning bodies of countless thousands. Then the whole sea turned to blood. The vision lasted about one hour." [8]

Jung chose to interpret the vision as a precognition of the First World War when it was in psychiatric terms a psychotic episode.

Jung was not just operating the simple defence mechanism of intellectualising what had happened. But surprisingly he took this even further because he began to think that his special insight and his understanding of the unconscious processes enabled him to prophesy the future. He was in a psychotic state and was obviously deluded, believing that he had prophetic powers.

Anthony Storr interviewed Jung on 14th April 1951. Storr was a respected English psychiatrist and author who was well known for his piercingly accurate psychoanalytical portraits of historical figures. He was convinced that Jung's experience during this four-year period was a severe and prolonged psychotic illness. Storr later reflected:

"Although I wrote earlier that I did not accept R.D Laing's theory that psychosis is a path to higher wisdom, there are a few cases of rather acute episodes of psychotic illness from which the patient emerges changed and perhaps enriched, and this sequence of events appears to be particularly common in those who become gurus because the revelation which enriches them forms the basis of their subsequent teaching. Jung certainly suffered from hallucinations and episodes of depersonalisation." [9]

A large part of Jung's four-year mental illness and recovery involved healing and reinventing himself. This obviously meant developing a coherent persona which was acceptable to the wider world.

His salvation was to develop his own theory of reality which gave rise to Analytical Psychology. He had broken away from not only his father's religion, but also from Freud. His life and work were an attempt to go beyond religion, to develop a secular form of salvation and perhaps heal the distress of his parent's wounds. He understood all too well the adage that 'what is not resolved will be repeated.'

Storr said when he met and interviewed him, Jung clearly believed that he was a prophet and a guru. Storr was fascinated by gurus and in his book *Feet of Clay* he examines with humane insight several flawed gurus such as Jim Koresh, George Gurdjieff, Rudolph Steiner, Bhagwan Shree Rajneesh, Jung, Sigmund Freud, Ignatius Loyola, Paul Brunton and Mother Meera. All of these spiritual teachers satisfied his criteria for being a guru. Storr was emphatic that Jung was a guru.

'What I'm writing now,' Jung told me *'is pure poison. But I owe it to my people.'*

'I was taken aback by this remark at the time,' writes Storr, 'for I knew that no ordinary psychiatrist would talk like that of 'my people': that is the statement of a guru. Jung's disciples might be few, but he had no doubts about his position.' [10]

Jung's perspective of himself as a prophetic guru would have made it very difficult if not impossible for him to meet Ramana Maharshi, who as a genuine guru would have called into question, albeit in silence, Jung's claim to be someone with the special abilities of an authentic guru.

It seems that Jung had only an intellectual understanding of Ramana Maharshi's practice of Self-enquiry resulting in the displacement of the ego by the atman, that is to say, 'the Self'. Jung argued that Ramana Maharshi might have transcended his ego or he may have endlessly struggled to annihilate it. [11]

Jung's error was to question Ramana Maharshi's state by

using psychological analysis, for psychology is a subject limited to the study of the mind. What Ramana Maharshi practically demonstrated transcends psychology because 'the Self' is beyond the mind. Jung admits this when he acknowledges that psychology is not competent to differentiate between God and 'the Self' being God. [12] Ramana Maharshi said that the 'Self,' Guru and God are all the same.

Jung says that his own field of psychology is not competent to understand 'the Self' in which Ramana Maharshi was merged. But what Jung does not say is very important. Jung never admits that he made any attempt to merge himself in 'the Self' as Ramana Maharshi did. In fact, he disparaged the notion that the loss of ego was either crucial or even feasible. This may explain in part, why he deliberately avoided meeting Ramana Maharshi.

Jung was at complete variance with Ramana Maharshi because he was a man of the mind, of expansive thinking, of new ideas. Jung believed we should have a healthy ego using mythology, archetypes, dream analysis and psychoanalysis to bring about Self Individuation as he calls it. His thinking mind was everything to him. Jung literally spoke volumes about this in his *Collected Works* and in his correspondence.

It is highly unlikely that Jung ever tried to actually practice Ramana Maharshi's Self-enquiry and perhaps he never even entertained the thought of doing this because it involved ignoring his ego, which would have been very threatening to his new intellectual belief system and secular form of salvation.

I suspect that Jung probably could not have afforded the risk of another long episode of psychosis and that most likely he got cold feet about meeting Ramana Maharshi. He had built up not just a reputation but a whole international following of disciples with him as the guru of a new psychology. This was the glue that held his ego together. With his history of a four year long psychotic illness Jung was not going to lose his sense of identity again. On a broader level, another interpretation could be that Jung thought his role was to reveal in the powerful myths of Western civilisation the means for redemption. Any interaction with Ramana Maharshi may have risked interfering with his chosen path.

Ramana Maharshi's message of Self-enquiry could be seen as a simple and practical way of immersion in 'the Self,' without all the apparatus of the new intellectual Analytical psychology Jung advocated. In the early days of psychology, Jung stated that he wasn't the sort of man to support anything he hadn't discovered himself. In his autobiography this is the fundamental reason for him being dismissive of the 'holy men' in India where he said that he had to find the truth out for himself. [13]

Jung was very serious about deliberately avoiding the 'holy men' especially one who would have jeopardised his life's work. He seemed closed to anyone else's vision of the truth. This is in keeping with Anthony Storr's criteria for him being a guru. One could postulate that Jung was not only arrogant and rigid about truth but also about what he claimed to actually know.

Although Jung referred to his ideas as a subjective confession and said that he did not want to force them

55

on others, there is no doubt that he believed that he had privileged access to a realm beyond consciousness. When John Freeman interviewed Jung in October 1959, he asked him:
'Do you believe in God?' Jung famously replied:
'I know.'

Anthony Storr wrote :
" 'When talking about dreams Jung said to me':
'Every night you have the chance of the Eucharist' and I have been told that the coterie of close disciples who knew him well waited hopefully every morning to hear if the great man had had another significant message from the unconscious." [14]

A long-term Dutch resident of Tiruvannamalai was Hamsananda J. J. de Reede or Hamsa as he was known. His mentor Dr Gualthernus Mees was a Dutch sociologist and a friend of Jung's. I rented a house from Hamsa on the lower slopes of Arunachala from the early 1980s and spoke several times with him. I remember well our first conversation.

"You told me that a friend of yours knew Jung very well."

"Yes. I was tortured in a POW camp in Java during the Second World War and was brought to the mountain to recover by another Dutchman called Dr Mees. Jung stayed at Dr Mees's house in Thiruvananthapuram during his visit to India. Jung kept in touch with Dr Mees after returning to Europe. I was the only beneficiary of Dr Mees estate and of course the house on the lower slopes of the mountain."

"Why do you think Jung didn't visit Tiruvannamalai?

"Well . . . apparently there was a lot of thought that he may have been overcome by Ramana, by his authenticity. You see Jung was a mystic and Ramana was 'an ordinary man'. Jung was fundamentally a psychological guru and a mystic."

What Jung wrote about Ramana Maharshi in his chapter 'The Holy Men of India' was originally used as an introduction to Zimmer's book *The Way to the Self*, [15] and this essay was heavily edited before it was used as the introduction to 'The Spiritual Teachings of Ramana Maharshi.' [16] This was almost certainly edited because certain people who were aware of Ramana Maharshi's authenticity probably saw that what Jung wrote about Ramana Maharshi was unacceptable because Jung seemed uncharacteristically ambivalent.

There is compelling evidence which shows there were several powerful forces influencing Jung at that time of his visit to India which discouraged him from visiting Ramana Maharshi. Understanding these forces explains his ambivalence in the chapter 'The Holy Men of India.' By examining Jung's ambivalence it is possible to penetrate his defences.

Jung's understanding of 'the Self' was only from an intellectual stance not from one of experiencing the atman 'the Self' through bliss-consciousness-existence, (Sat Chit Ananda). Jung borrowed ideas from the East about the atman, 'the Self' but when he was presented with the opportunity of being face to face with Ramana Maharshi, an authentic guru, he studiously avoided meeting him.

He describes Ramana Maharshi as being absorbed in 'the Self' but admits to not understanding Ramana Maharshi's Self-realisation or his significance. He also admits that his field of psychology is not competent in understanding the Eastern insight of the atman 'the Self'. This begs the question, 'Why exactly was Jung, who was a psychologist, so critical?' When we look at his later correspondence, it proves that Jung concealed the truth about why he didn't meet Ramana Maharshi and why his description of Ramana Maharshi vacillated in the chapter 'The Holy Men of India.'

In later correspondence, Jung confesses that he was clearly aware of the profound danger he would be in if he delved further into the East. It is only logical to extrapolate on this that the person who represented the gravest risk to Jung of losing his bearings for a second time, was the person he wrote the most about in the East and that was Ramana Maharshi. He pointed out that he knew only too well the price he might have to pay to restore himself to what he had been before.

In a Letter to Countess Elizabeth Klinckowstroem Jung says that he just had to accept being content with his European assumptions about Eastern philosophy because although he thought Eastern philosophy filled a void in people, it was too dangerous for him to personally explore. This can only refer to his first psychotic breakdown:

'I would be in danger of losing my roots for a second time.' He writes, *'This is something I would rather not risk.'* [17]

Many of Jung's comments about why he didn't visit Ramana Maharshi seem so uncharacteristically overcritical and unbalanced that they leave you wondering if

58

Shakespeare's perceptions of people might be appropriate here, "The lady doth protest too much methinks." [18] This means that one can insist so passionately about something being true that people suspect the opposite of what you are saying. That has always been my suspicion about Jung. My conclusion is that Jung regrettably got cold feet, which might have been appropriate, but which sadly resulted in him missing a golden opportunity.

Jung never doubted Ramana Maharshi's authenticity but he did question his uniqueness. Time has shown Jung to be quite wrong about this. The truth is that they were both important. Each served a purpose in the spiritual development of humanity. Jung was a psychiatrist who behaved like a prophet and a guru.

Jung made advantageous use of his bouts of psychotic illness to deepen his experience and make valuable contributions to psychology. Whatever the defects of his essay, in the chapter, 'The Holy Men of India,' he did bring attention to Ramana Maharshi, which may turn out to be much more important than we realise.

Lastly, in comparing the two the final proof lies in simply looking at how the two men were when their lives ended. Did they die happy? Despite the excruciating pain of the sarcoma Ramana Maharshi left this world serene. There were tears of joy in his eyes as his devotees chanted 'Arunachala Siva'.

But sadly it, seems rather tragic that Jung did not appear to have found that elixir, the permanent transformative happiness. This is most clearly seen in Claire Dunne's compassionate account of Jung's life.

In his last few days, Marie-Louise von Franz visited Jung and confirmed that he was still having visions:

"When I last saw him he had a vision. Jung said that he saw vast parts of the Earth devastated. [19]

His final mental state and the path he died travelling on are also penetratingly described by someone else who knew him at that time. Miguel Serrano, a Chilean writer who formed a friendship late in Jung's life commented:

"Up until the last moment Jung still seemed to be searching. Perhaps his was the road of the magician who, unlike the saint, did not yearn for fusion or for peace of God, but preferred the eternal highway with all its unhappiness." [20]

It is important to understand that both Jung and Ramana Maharshi were pioneers who revivified ancient teachings that had either been lost or corrupted. Both rediscovered, in their own inimitable ways, treasures which can heal and guide us.

Fundamental to his Analytical Psychology he re-invigorated the paradigm of the four psychological functions: thinking, feeling, sensation and intuition. Jung borrowed these from the astrological four elements of air, earth, fire and water which astrology uses to classify the twelve personality types into four groups. He also introduced the concepts of complexes, Introversion/Extroversion.

He explored new fields of study going beyond dream psychology leading to research into alchemy and astrology. That is to say, leading to new avenues in the eternal quest for Self-knowledge.

Carl Jung arrived on the scene when the myths of the gods were no longer given credence and the Western soul was dying from the insidious vacuum of disbelief and cynicism. One could say he was the new Parsifal in search of the Holy Grail.

The final success alluded him. When he died he was still asking questions. He was a magus who dedicated his heart and mind to the eternal search.

Ramana Maharshi on the other hand dedicated his life to 'just being.' In this he recharged the noble tradition of Advaita Vedanta. His perception remained razor-sharp, free of all pre-conceptions.

It is more than likely that in the future Ramana Maharshi's legacy will yield a far greater understanding of the nature of 'the Self' than we have at this time. Meanwhile many benefit from absorbing his teaching and practicing his method of 'Self-enquiry' of just being. Many also benefit from visiting his shrine where his presence is still felt.

What would have transpired if Ramana Maharshi and Carl Jung had met remains in the realm of counterfactual speculation. Perhaps this is something to be discussed elsewhere. But this we do know, that even though their paths did not meet, the impact of India and its philosophy which permeates the way of life in India profoundly influenced Jung and the development of his insights into human consciousness.

They both lived at the same time and took different paths to seek their own happiness. One took a silent inner path of stillness, the other a vocal outer intellectual path of knowledge.

They both demonstrated that either way requires commitment and perseverance. Just as each must find his or her own path.

We have seen that one died in happiness whilst the other died still searching for it.

According to the American psychiatrist Gerald Jampolsky:

"You can be right or you can be happy." [21]

Personally, I prefer the second of Jampolsky's options.

Being happy or right are options to which we will give further attention.

7.

Thought, stillness and happiness

'It is a blessing to be born into a religion and a tragedy to die in one'

Unknown

7.

Thought, stillness and happiness

'You can be right or you can be happy'

Gerald Jampolsky

One reason Carl Jung is a good point of reference is that he wrote so much about himself and divulged a great deal about what drove him.

The intent is not to be dismissive of Carl Jung but rather to use the information he gave us about himself in a meaningful way. It is largely through the vast written legacy of Carl Jung about himself that we can explore this area.

A great deal of Carl Jung's theories come from his own story and have been taken up and used as maps for others to follow. Some of his ideas and models may well help us to understand ourselves whilst others may be too intellectual and actually lead us away from the path to 'the Self.' Carl Jung said that psychology did not have the capability to explain 'the Self.' [1]

This suggests that for those people who are predominantly 'thinkers' it is more difficult to actually understand and follow the path to the 'the Self.' and experience it. Carl Jung wrote a great deal about using thinking to interpret almost everything and he helped us to understand many things better. He wrote very extensively and intelligently around the subject of the 'the Self' but later he admitted that he was too vulnerable to actually look inwards and discover it. [2]

The significance of this is that it illustrates that there can be real practical difficulties in enquiring into and practising spirituality and particularly Eastern spiritual disciplines. This is a very significant psychological admission for Carl Jung and for us. Why should this be so? There are probably at least two major explanations.

It seems that a large proportion of people find it difficult or are unable to actually practice and get in touch with the 'the Self.' It also seems that some people avoid looking for 'the Self.' Perhaps it is because of fear. They feel they are too vulnerable and fragile.'

Both can result in what looks like someone getting stuck over-thinking about 'the Self' without being able to get on and do it. It looks like they are hovering over the literature on the subject and circling around the facts and guidance without actually being able to put the experience into practice. It is like someone who cannot ride a bike talking about how to improve your bike riding skills.

I am going to use Carl Jung's own narrative to show how his inability to get in touch with and experience 'the Self' also reflected an over cerebral man who was in point of fact unconsciously childish in dealing with other people.

Jung is an example of someone who is reluctant to approach 'the Self,' because of difficulties which might lead to mental illness. He is also as an example of being over- intellectual and not being able to actually 'just be still.'

Carl Jung said that psychology lacks the competence to understand 'the Self' and so the mind is not the best instrument to examine it. Just being still is a level of conscious awareness which is usually obscured by the mind. 'Just being still' is a much more subtle state of consciousness. Both are not equally open to our consciousness because one is simply obscured by the other: essentially 'the Self ' by the mind. Awareness of 'the Self' can only occur when the mind is empty. Only practice reveals this veiling by the mind. 'The Self' has to be experienced practically.

'The Self' has to be experienced. At some stage this requires a practical leap from thinking about 'the Self' to trying to experience 'just being still.' To just be still and shut down thinking requires effort, commitment and practice.

Over-thinking or being over-intellectual may result from being conditioned to think all of the time both at home and in education, and it is a very common condition. Overthinking can also be a way to compensate for not being able to get in touch with one's feelings. This is because feelings can be awkward and painful.

Those who mainly seem to see things intellectually can be prone to getting blocked and stuck on an intellectual level. This can happen when trying to understand all kinds of things, but especially when trying to understand something like 'the Self.'

This form of mental constipation is not only getting stuck and blocked in thinking, it is also an obstacle to any practical progress along the inner path. This is common especially in the bright clever type of person, perhaps because of over-conditioning.

Are there people who are more 'thinking types' and much more intellectual? Carl Jung's mind is an interesting example to observe here, first because he was very bright and second because he describes his own 'type' very honestly.

Let us digress for a moment to take a deeper look at the very nature of Carl Jung in how he presented this material. The point here is to illustrate how totally controlled and driven he was by thinking and knowledge.

In his 'Psychological Types' [3] which was published in 1921, Jung was one of the first modern psychologists to suggest a useful way of re-classifying the various personality types. Jung probably borrowed the idea of his Four Functions: Thinking, Feeling, Sensation, and Intuition from both astrology and the Greek physician, Galen's (c.190 CE) Four Humours of Sanguine, Melancholic, Choleric and Phlegmatic.

Galen had taken these from Hippocrates' (c.370 BCE) original idea of the Four Temperaments: Blood, Phlegm, Yellow Bile, and Black Bile. These were the ancient Greeks' way of classifying the different temperaments or personality types and also astrology's way of dividing the twelve signs of the Zodiac into the Four Elements of Earth, Air, Fire and Water to reflect the nature of the four fundamental personality types.

Jung had a great interest in astrology in which the twelve signs of the Zodiac are divided into four categories. These reflect the nature of the four fundamental personality types. Jung, as has been said, was of course, a very keen disciple of astrology. The four ancient traditional basic types obviously predate Jung by many centuries. In his volume 'Psychological Types,' Carl Jung describes the four basic types outlined above at extraordinary length. He uses the first 329 pages of the 608 pages to look at their origins and the history of the four elements, which even by today's standards could seem excessively over-intellectual. However, Carl Jung was one of the very early researchers in the new discipline of psychology. Most research today involves quoting multiple sources, just as Carl Jung did.

In the words of the American Playwright Wilson Mizner, 'To steal ideas from one person is plagiarism; to steal from many is research.' We will return to the area of plagiarism later.

Our observation of what knowledge and what 'knowing' is about is not yet complete. It is worth pursuing just a little further. The point is simply to illustrate Carl Jung's total dedication if not obsession with thinking and in particular 'knowing.' What follows shows that Carl Jung had a passionate dedication to knowledge. He also had an unresolved lifelong obsession about not being a plagiarist. It is worth watching the 1959 BBC interview titled, 'Face to Face,' Carl Gustav Jung,' by John Freeman, who had been thoroughly briefed by my psychotherapy teacher Anthony Storr, who knew Jung personally. [4] The interview is on the internet.

Even in his eighties when talking about the school master who accused him of plagiarism 60-70 years earlier, Jung becomes animated, gets irritated and loses his composure, striking the table many times. His usual impeccable English becomes faulty.

Concentrate on the sound and listen to him tapping the table at first, then hitting the table with increasing force and frequency, in timing with the crescendo of his anger. It is as if all his wounds from his childhood remain unhealed and as fresh as if they had just happened. Perhaps it is good to watch the video two or three times. Here is as transcription of part of the interview:

JF: 'And did you, when you decided to become a doctor, have difficulty getting the training at school and passing the exams?'

CJ: 'I particularly had a difficulty with a certain teacher that didn't believe that I could write a decent thesis. I remember one case where the teacher had the person to discuss the paper written by the pupils and he took the best first and he went through the whole number of the pupils and I didn't appear and I was badly troubled and worried. I just thought well it is impossible that this thesis could be that bad. And when he had finished, he said,'

"There is still one paper left over and that is the one by Carl Jung. That would be by far the best paper if it hadn't been copied. He has, he has just copied it somewhere, stolen. You are a thief you, and if I knew where you had, have stolen it you, you, you, I would fling you out to school."

'And I, I went mad and I, I said, This is the one thesis where I have worked the most because the theme was interesting in contradistinction you know to other things which are not at all interesting to me.' And then he said, "You are a liar and if you can prove that you have stolen that thing so then you get out of school." [sic] (It is interesting at this point Jung loses control of his usually correct English.)

70

'Now that was a very serious thing to me because what else then? You see and I hated that fellow and that was the, the only man I could have killed you know if I had met him once at a dark corner. I would have shown him some, something of what I can do.'

JF: 'Did you often have violent thoughts about people when you were young?'

An analyst is not needed to understand Jung's problem. Astonishingly even in his eighties Carl Jung had completely unresolved issues about his thinking, knowledge, power and violence. He was not only uninhibited but also unconscious and rather childishly immature. Over half a century earlier he had written one of the most important papers on plagiarism (Cryptomnesia, in 1905) [5]. Yet this knowledge seemed to be of no use to him when he recalls being accused of being a plagiarist.

His outrage was quite extraordinary and in total contrast to Robert Louis Stevenson's humility and open embarrassment when he discovered years later after writing 'Treasure Island' that he had unwittingly plagiarized Tales of a Traveller by Washington Irving which he had read as a child. Stevenson writes:

'It is my debt to Washington Irving that exercises my conscience, and justly so, for I believe plagiarism was rarely carried farther. I chanced to pick up the Tales of a Traveller some years ago with a view to an anthology of prose narrative, and the book flew up and struck me: Billy Bones, his chest, the company in the parlour, the whole inner spirit, and a good deal of the material detail of my first chapters — all were there, all were the property of

Washington Irving.'

It is an interesting point that Carl Jung's years of looking outside for knowledge seemed to have failed to have changed him and bring him fulfilment.

Now to return to Carl Jung's model of human types for a moment. Although he suggested that a person was either Introverted or Extroverted, essentially Carl Jung's model of personality is based on a person making decisions by either being a Thinking or a Feeling type and also gathering information by either being a Sensation type or an Intuition type. Carl Jung suggested that each person has one of each pair of these qualities dominant in their personality.

The reason for mentioning all of this is that Carl Jung shows us what we have known for thousands of years, which is that a large proportion of people are like the element of air and are probably thinking types, whereas others are the opposite, water or feeling types. This can partly explain why so many people who are the more 'thinking types' seem to get blocked in trying to follow the path of getting in touch with 'the Self,' as described by Ramana Maharshi. This is so because in uncovering 'the Self,' the mind has to be completely relegated. This is more difficult for the 'thinking types' because they are accustomed to giving precedence to their minds. Again, Carl Jung is himself an excellent example of this.

I have already mentioned one particular question in the Freeman interview. But it is now worth returning to it and looking at it from a different position. Freeman asks Carl Jung a direct question which again reveals the extent of Carl Jung's over-thinking and that he was characterised by being obsessed with thinking rather than with any other mode of perception.

JF: 'Do you believe in God?'

CJ: 'Now? Difficult to answer. I know. I don't need to believe. I know.'

This was a very unusual thing to say which drew some interest from the public. Although Carl Jung spent most of his life trying to go beyond religion, from his vast textbook knowledge about religion, most practising monks would almost certainly say it is extremely unlikely that facts from books would enable anyone to say in relation to God "I know."

When Carl Jung said he didn't need to believe, this was not correct because he spent most of his life searching for knowledge to create a system of thought that he and others could believe in. Perhaps he was simply using thinking and knowing to avoid what he terms 'the unconscious,' which for him was a terrifying part of him just beneath the surface. But for others whose thinking is not such a potential area of loss of control, there is the lure for 'just being still,' 'the Self.'

Again, when Freeman asks Carl Jung about himself, Carl Jung confirms exactly what category of person he is. It is worth listening to this recording. Here is a transcription of the recording.

JF: 'Have you concluded what psychological type you are yourself?

CJ: 'Naturally I have devoted a great deal of attention to

that painful question, you know.'

JF: 'And reached a conclusion?'

CJ: 'Well you see the type is nothing static. It changes in the course of life but I was most certainly characterised by thinking. I always thought from early childhood on. And I had a great deal of intuition too, and I had a definite difficulty with feeling and my relation to reality was not particularly brilliant. I was often at variance with the reality of things. Now that gives you all the necessary data.'

In contrast, Ramana Maharshi also spent over 50 years practicing, but in silence staying with what he had found as a young man through his method of Self-enquiry. The obvious difference between the two men is the outcome as Carl Jung was searching up until the last moment.[6] Ramana Maharshi was at peace with himself and completely fulfilled for over fifty years. It is therefore appropriate to conclude with what he said about knowledge and happiness in 'Who am I?' when he was about twenty-two years old. [7]

Question 23: 'Is it any use reading books for those who long for release?'

M.: 'All the texts say that in order to gain release one should render the mind quiescent; therefore their conclusive teaching is that the mind should be rendered quiescent; once this has been understood there is no need for endless reading. In order to quieten the mind one has only to enquire within oneself what one's Self is; how could this search be done in books?

One should know one's Self with one's own eye of wisdom.

The Self is within the five sheaths; but books are outside them. Since the Self has to be enquired into by discarding the five sheaths, it is futile to search for it in books. There will come a time when one has to forget all that one has learnt.'

Question 24. 'What is happiness?'

M.: 'Happiness is the very nature of Self; happiness and the Self are not different. There is no happiness in any object of the world. We imagine through our ignorance that we derive happiness from objects. When the mind goes out, it experiences misery. In truth, when its desires are fulfilled, it returns to its own place and enjoys the happiness that is the Self. Similarly in the states of sleep, Samadhi, and fainting and when the object desired is obtained or the object disliked is removed, the mind becomes inward-turned and enjoys pure Self-happiness. Thus the mind moves without rest, alternately going out of the Self and returning to it.

Under the tree the shade is pleasant; out in the open the heat is scorching. A person who has been going about in the sun feels cool when he reaches the shade. Someone who keeps on going from the shade into the sun and then back into the shade is a fool. A wise man stays permanently in the shade. Similarly, the mind of the one who knows the truth does not leave Brahman.

The mind of the ignorant, on the contrary, revolves in the world, feeling miserable, and for a little time returns to Brahman to experience happiness. In fact, what is called the world is only thought. When the world disappears, i.e. when there is no thought, the mind experiences happiness;

and when the world appears, it goes through misery.'

Over forty years later he was asked the same question. [8]

Talk 3. A question was asked as to the nature of happiness.

M.: If a man thinks that his happiness is due to external causes and his possessions, it is reasonable to conclude that his happiness must increase with the increase of possessions and diminish in proportion to their diminution. Therefore if he is devoid of possessions, his happiness should be nil. What is the real experience of man? Does it conform to this view? In deep sleep the man is devoid of possessions, including his own body. Instead of being unhappy he is quite happy. Everyone desires to sleep soundly. The conclusion is that happiness is inherent in man and is not due to external causes. One must realise his Self in order to open the store of unalloyed happiness.

The contrast between Carl Jung and Ramana Maharshi typifies the apparent irreconcilability of the intellectual quest for knowledge of 'the Self' with the direct inner approach to subdue unwanted thought in order to attain bliss.

8.

Mutual Aid Groups

'The Way Out is In'

Thich Nhat Hanh

8.

Mutual Aid Groups

Many people with addictions such as alcohol or drugs shy away from seeking help in 12-step mutual aid groups because they wrongly assume the groups to be religious and based on God. Let me try and clear this up with an anonymous quote . . .

'Religion is for people who are scared of going to Hell
Spirituality is for those who have been there'

The emphasis in these groups is not on religion but on each person's sense of their own higher power which could even be the group itself.

With that common block hopefully cleared away we may now discuss the paradox of how 'The Way Out is In.'

In todays society it seems more and more people are becoming addicted to various things. They are never satisfied with what they have and want more and more without ever becoming satisfied.

Some addictions are so commonplace that they are acceptable to the point that in many cases it is now politically incorrect to even mention them.

It could be someone's apparent need to always be on the phone, to constantly use a computer or to play computer games, to have more virtual friends or to gamble. It could also be that someone wants to control their appearance by weight loss, weight gain or by other cosmetic means.

Modern society has expanded the range of addictions so much that they now include a vast range of behaviours.

Let us alphabetise only the most common ones: anorexia, alcohol, bulimia, body building, cocaine, chocolate, crime, drugs not prescribed but available on the street such as glue, inhalants, solvents and legal highs, exercise, food, fetishes, gambling, heroin, internet, jogging, kleptomania, love, marijuana, nicotine, overeating, pornography, prescription drugs, quintessential behaviour (perfectionism), religion, social media, shopping, sex, self-harm, telephones, television, tattooing, under-achieving, video games, wealth, X-rated movies, yoga and Zzzzzzz sleep.

The naked truth behind addiction is dependence on the presumption that happiness comes solely from the exterior material world. Over-emphasis on the external World makes it much more difficult for people to access their inner selves.

Thinking or rationalism has led to insatiable cravings for external things and inner life has been neglected.

How has this come about? Our superficial externalised cultures promote and encourage the acquisition of certain behaviours, experiences and possessions through all kinds of
advertisements in the media using powerful role models.

Many of these create desires which when fulfilled give the illusion of having obtained the accepted symbols of success. Some of these create the craving for more.

Similarly, people's appetite for technological novelties in the external world is fuelled by desire for external knowledge so that they can alter the external world and satisfy their incessant cravings.

This is at the expense of their inner being. The desire of the mind to be dominant in everything overcomes their inner Self which is eclipsed and consequently withers. This results in a fatal loss of balance between the mind and the spirit. The inner 'spiritual' world is the glue which when shared holds groups of men and women together and so when it is dissolved people become isolated and unhappy. This is when they let addictions take hold.

On their last meeting in 1931, after nearly a year of daily therapy sessions, Carl Jung informed his patient Rowland H. of his 'hopelessness' as far as medical or psychiatric treatment was concerned in treating his addiction to alcohol.

Bluntly, Jung wrote him off, making him conscious of his powerlessness over his addiction. However, he said there might be hope for him if he became the subject of a religious experience or if he placed himself in the walls of a human community.

At first it seems that in 1931 Carl Jung was the first modern doctor to realise that medicine does not work for curing addictions. However, Temperance groups in the USA had known about this since the formation of the Washington Temperance Society (The Washingtonians) in the Chase's Tavern in Baltimore in 1840. Jung had visited America in December 1924 and it is highly unlikely he would not have known about the Washingtonians, all the more because Abraham Lincoln had been a supporter of the Washingtonians.

Jung's advice to Roland H. in 1931 was insightful and appeared ground-breaking. But did Jung derive the concept of mutual aid recovery from the American Washingtonians whom he would almost certainly have heard of during his visit to America in 1924?

Rowland H. helped a fellow American Bill Wilson to recover and in 1935 Wilson along with Dr Robert Smith went on to co-found Alcoholics Anonymous (AA). Bill Wilson said his conversation with Rowland H. his humility and deep perception played a critical role in the founding of the AA Fellowship.

In 1961, just months before Jung's death, Wilson wrote to thank Jung for his help in curing him of his addiction and his influence in helping to set up the first addiction recovery programme. [1]

Jung immediately replied informing him that he had taken a risk at the time in advising Rowland H. that the only hope left for him was to lead a spiritually based life in a community. [2] He said he could not have risked at that time telling Rowland H. more in case he was misunderstood. This is worth looking at in more detail later.

Most people believe that Jung's chief legacy was Analytical Psychology; a perspective which he hoped would take people further than religion in understanding themselves and making themselves whole. Some countries have Jungian groups or Jungian societies. These ideas and theories continue to exert a great deal of influence. Although Jung has been an important contributor to modern psychology his Analytical Psychology was not taken up by the medical or psychological establishments and never became mainstream. His actual practical influence on humankind has been quite different to what he expected. It took place just before he died and it has primarily been in the field of supporting mutual aid in curing addictions.

Accessing the Spirit

There are two ways of accessing the spirit; either the illusion of the spirit is invoked by excessively indulging in alcohol, drugs, eating, gambling and sex. Or the authentic spirit is invoked by the collapse of the ego and its surrender to the true Self. This is the true sense of the sacred.

Initially the lure of addiction gives people the feeling of satisfaction and wholeness whilst in reality they are isolated and fragmented. They are experiencing not genuine wholeness of spirit but an imitation, a 'cuckoo' spirit. [3]

The cuckoo is a parasitic bird which in ten seconds can push an egg out of a nest and lay one of its own there to be hatched and nurtured by the host bird. When the cuckoo chick hatches it supplants the other chicks and is usually a giant compared to them causing massive problems to the host mother. At first the host mother nurtures the cuckoo. This avine struggle for survival has similarities to the human arms race. The next time she lays eggs the host mother reacts by changing the pattern on her eggs so that she can recognise them as her own, as opposed to the imitation egg placed there by a cuckoo.

Compulsive Behaviour

Similar to the host mother feeding the cuckoo chick, addicts are aware that they are harming themselves, but are compelled to continue to satisfy their craving. Likewise, their families and friends continue to support them even though they know that addiction harms them as well.

When people gather together, having decided to fight their addiction, a spirit is formed in the group which is a higher power which no individual can develop on their own.

Just as the host mother uses nature to create an egg pattern which the cuckoo cannot mimic, the spirit of solidarity formed and experienced in a community can shatter the illusion of satisfaction and wholeness that addictions create.

A supportive, nurturing community which encourages togetherness, understanding and spiritual meaning can inspire hope and encourage addicts to want to change their behaviours and belong more to the community. For many this may be the only path available to a sense of authentic wholeness. There is no actual cure, no medicine or therapy but there is hope.

This possibility of hope given to addicts by Jung in the form of spirituality in a group has probably had more influence on the world in the form of addiction groups than all of his work. It has probably contributed more to the healing of the sick than any form of psychological therapy. His eventual contribution to mankind's spiritual development has been significant in a very different way to that which he imagined. It was not one on one psychotherapy but mutual aid in groups. Therapy may be useful after recovery has started but on its own will not bring about a meaningful recovery from addictions as Jung and many since him have indicated.

The most successful answers are in 12 step mutual aid groups such as 'Al-Anon' the mutual aid support group for family members of alcoholics or anyone affected by some else's addictive drinking provides an anonymous forum to share with others their experience, strength and hope. For many, this may be their most important source of help, just as Alcoholics Anonymous (AA) is for alcoholics, where 24% remain sober after five years and for many no other therapy may be necessary. Similar support groups exist for other specific problems such as people with eating disorders in Eating Disorders Anonymous (EDA). Eating disorders are the most lethal of mental illnesses with the highest
mortality rate.

There are also groups for those with sex addiction in Sex Addiction Anonymous (SAA) and those addicted to gambling in Gamblers Anonymous (GA). In addition to this there are free mutual aid support groups for people addicted to drugs such as cocaine in Narcotics Anonymous (NA) and those addicted to cannabis in Marijuana Anonymous (MA).

The Wider External World

The devastation is nowhere more obvious than in most of the native populations of North America and Australia whose spirit is still enshrined in their lands which they can no longer freely access. This is also becoming true in Tibet and in other lands where the natives' traditional connections with their sense of the spiritual through the earth are severed.

Relocation, poverty, poor education, lack of prospects and opportunities could each be named as the culprit behind their addictions but this is not the original and ongoing cause.

The true reason is that they have had their spiritual connection with the earth removed and they have had it replaced with a substitution of a false spirit composed of drugs or alcohol usually supplied by the thief who took their original true sense of wholeness and sacred integrity, a cuckoo spirit.

The cuckoo spirit also inhabits and deeply affects family members and friends, disguising and taking over their true spirit.

It seems as if addiction has been weaponised to overcome whole nations which once flourished on and were proud of their moral integrity and spiritual life.

The diet of the soul seems to have been overpowered by man's greed to obtain, own and control.

Families and Friends

Whatever the origin, addictions are a progressive disease infecting all of the addicts' relationships. Addictions cannot be controlled or cured, only arrested.

Addiction is not just an individual illness. Everyone in the family is deeply affected and unhappy.

In some areas, whole communities and nations of people are deeply affected by addictions. Every family member leads a depleted life through the illusion that they can control the addict. Nevertheless, they keep on trying to change and control the addict.

In trying to change the addict's behaviour family members change emotionally. They become emotionally disturbed, often without realising it.

They get stuck in a cycle of trying to control something which is unmanageable. They feel that they are being driven crazy.

There are similar patterns in all addicts and their families. The addict's effect on everyone is chaotic and unpredictable with the result that everyone feels powerless.

Unlike other diseases, addiction is unmanageable and the people around the addict have to be over-vigilant. They cannot relax in normal ways and therefore cannot relate in normal ways. They often become obsessional.

Family members and friends become different in the sense that they are not free to be their 'full selves.'

They remain emotionally confined and limited by the addicted person's behaviour. As well as fear and shame there is always resentment and anger.

Unless family members are helped, this pattern of damage

usually continues in their relationships with all others and extends for their whole life. Similarly, drug addiction/ alcoholism not only devastates families, but also the next generation of children whose parents are handicapped because they themselves were brought up by an addicted parent.

Addicts may remain addicted as an emotional anaesthetic because they do not have the tools and the skills that are necessary to deal with emotions.

Often, they are unable to handle their emotions. They were not taught to do so because they were brought up in an environment by a close relative who was an addict who was emotionally out of control.

Detachment

it is only when a point of desperation is reached that their 'hopelessness' is recognised and help is sought.

The well-meaning efforts of family members can even prevent addicts from getting the help they so desperately need.

It is as if there has to be a rock bottom 'gutter moment.' Likewise, there may be a 'gutter moment' for family members and friends when they feel they will go crazy unless they leave the relationship or get some help.

The naked truth about this time is best seen and understood by a parallel example in nature, as told in the following story.

A young boy found a chrysalis and knowing what was inside it he brought it into his house where he waited for it to open up. He waited for hours looking at the chrysalis waiting for the butterfly to open it and emerge.

He eventually fell asleep and woke in the morning to find a hole had appeared in the chrysalis. He watched it for a long time and finally in the afternoon a black leg appeared out of a hole struggling to make the hole bigger.

There was little progress by the evening and so the boy thought he would help. He went to his Granny's sewing basket where he found a delicate pair of scissors that she used for crochet work. He went back to the chrysalis. where the leg was still struggling to open it. He delicately cut a line along the opening and out emerged the creature.

He looked at it for a long time waiting for it to open its wings but it just seemed to wriggle about. Eventually he placed it by the open window where he thought the air would help it.

He went off to ask his Granny for her help. She came back with him but the creature was lying on its back with its legs straight in the air as if dead.

His Granny said, "When a butterfly is trying to get out of its chrysalis, it struggles so hard that its heart beats faster and faster until its blood pressure gets very high. The very high pressure forces blood into the wings so that they open up, thus breaking open the chrysalis. It is the only way a butterfly's wings can open."

The loved ones of drug addicts and alcoholics usually support their illnesses and cover up for all of their mistakes and shortcomings. But this only prolongs and prevents the addict and their family from getting proper help. Family and friends think they can control and cure the addictions but they are unmanageable diseases which can only be arrested.

Referring an addict for medical or psychological help usually wastes time because most doctors, psychiatrists and psychotherapists are not experts in this area.

The proof that recovering addicts themselves are the experts and the most efficacious in helping other stop using alcohol or drugs is simply that they are 'clean' and sober.

Any other therapy is usually either a waste of time or will only delay access to Narcotics/Alcoholics Anonymous. They might as well go straight to Narcotics/Alcoholics Anonymous to start with.

The drug addict/alcoholic may have some other problems which can be helped by therapy but this can only happen later on. The primary problem must be spelt out and acted on first; otherwise, it risks, and may encourage, denial and avoidance and can perpetuate the problem.

A person who goes to Narcotics Anonymous or Alcoholics Anonymous will learn something that they can learn no other way.

Most drug addicts or alcoholics who stop taking drugs or alcohol without using the resources offered for support and development by groups like Narcotics Anonymous,

Alcoholics Anonymous remain as fragmented addicts or sober drunks who crave alcohol or drugs. Usually, their block in going to Narcotics/Alcoholics Anonymous is obsessional fear simply due to their lack of emotional tools and skills. Ironically Narcotics/Alcoholics Anonymous is just the place where they will find these emotional tools.

Similarly, anyone who has had to suffer and endure living with a drug addict/alcoholic is usually wounded on so many levels of consciousness that there is no point in thinking they can get adequate help from well-meaning doctors, psychologists and psychotherapists.

They are best helped by the friends and families of other drug addicts/alcoholics who have worked through this and who are therefore experts. They offer hope that there is a way out for families and friends to avoid being overwhelmed by a drug addict/alcoholic and their disease.

Families and friends need to understand how to deal with their emotions and their sense of their 'inner Self'. They need to look again with another 'understanding family' to try to see the drug addiction/alcoholism with loving non-attachment. They can then reconnect with others, their 'inner Self' and their sense of the sacred. Their boundaries, attitudes and relationships can then at last begin to improve as they recover.

Recovery

The prospect of recovery is based on four principal ideas. The first is that as an addict or a family member you are utterly 'powerless' over drugs, alcohol or any other addiction.

The second is that because of this the only option is to turn to something bigger than yourself... your sense of a higher power or the sacred. For some this higher power may be just the power of the group they go to.

The third is realising that your thinking, attitudes and behaviours have been conditioned by the addict. You also accept that you want to change.

The fourth is that you can only keep the gift of healing that you have received if you give it away by helping others.

Perhaps the most liberating principle of mutual aid 12 step programmes for addictions is freedom from religious dogma.

This more unifying inclusive approach has been echoed repeatedly . . .

'Religion is for people who are scared of going to Hell.
Spirituality is for those who have been there'

9.

Spirit against Spirit

'The happy stillness of being we look for
Is not freedom from pain and suffering
But it is amidst pain and suffering.'

9.

Spirit against Spirit

'Criticism or just silence can be a mask hiding fear, envy or ignorance'

In all walks of life many people hide what they see as their goal of success. Their goal may be more important than being openly truthful, transparent and helpful. They are usually motivated by money, power or the adulation of their ego being seen in some special way as important.

Whether we are looking for a doctor, therapist or guru, we need to be careful and be on our guard.

Therapists, doctors and gurus are fundamentally the same as everyone else in this respect and frequently do not act with our best interests at heart. Like anyone, they may be motivated only to promote their own interests aiming to acquire money, power and prestige.

Carl Jung was not only a doctor and a therapist but he also regarded himself as a Guru. When we need help, in trying to assess what we need and who we should ask for help, Jung is an early example of us needing to separate out these overlapping fields. Do we need a doctor, a therapist, a guru, a mutual aid self help group or even a friend?

Jung came from a long family line of religious pastors and as a teenager he was sexually abused by one of his family's male friends. He did not reveal if the perpetrator was a religious pastor. However, most of Jung's professional life was concerned with going beyond religion with his own new brand of belief called 'Analytical Psychology.'

To do this he used his own personal experience of his long psychotic illness and to achieve maximum credibility he mixed it with knowledge from many fields such as history, mythology, astrology, medicine and psychology.

He put this his thoughts in his Opus Magnum, a large collection of perhaps overintellectual volumes known as the 'Collected Works' which can at best be described as woolly. The Red Book his personal 'Biblical' style book, locked away in a safe on his instructions for decades after his death can only be described as his personal account of psychosis.

Jung's attempt to go beyond religion with his own brand of Analytical Psychology was not popular and was not widely taken up by either doctors or psychologists. His attempt to introduce a new way of classifying people into 'Psychological Types' was also flawed. However, Jung travelled to many corners of the world giving lectures, presenting papers, appearing on the radio and television for decades presenting his version of truth. He seemed to be in search of recognition and veneration.

In order to maintain his acknowledged position Jung seemed to hide, disguise, not mention or only slightly criticise any spiritual path which he saw as being in competition with his new psychological path of Analytical Psychology. This is not immediately obvious.

Jung's masterly selective omissions of other spiritual paths during the thirty years 1931-1961 could have deceptively blocked and prevented the discovery of two important spiritual paths based on ancient wisdom which might have otherwise eclipsed his own popularity. One was originally from Ancient Rome: Bill Wilson's Alcoholics Anonymous. The other was from India: Ramana Maharshi's path of Self -enquiry. Both were blossoming at exactly the same time as Carl Jung's new Analytical Psychology in the three decades from 1930-1960.

Instead of contributing on a spiritual level to mankind, Jung attempted to conceal genuine spirituality on a large scale. This was in order to enhance his own prestige as a psychological leader. Jung was an intellectual and contributed much to the understanding of religion and the development of the new field of psychology. However, it seems he may have wanted the adulation of being a world-famous psychological guru more than being openly truthful and transparent.

As we have seen Jung's attempts to conceal the importance of Ramana Maharshi's silent stillness did not work. He avoided visiting Ramana Maharshi. He did not recognise or acknowledge the direct path to the Self which was demonstrated and quietly taught in silence by Ramana Maharshi.

When questioned about this after he returned from India, he wrote a whole chapter 'The Holy Men of India' ducking, diving and dodging the real issue of feeling his professional importance and personal integrity threatened by the presence of Ramana Maharshi. Perhaps because of his earlier illness he needed the feeling of security. He found himself in a position where he had to choose between his intellectually based ego or the happiness of inner stillness. The two things do not sit together.

Jung's distancing himself from Ramana Maharshi was only one example of attempts to conceal the importance of other spiritual paths. Jung also managed to conceal and ignore the important insight that mutual aid can help people recover from addictions and compulsive behaviours.

Jung hid the importance of spiritual groups in recovery from addictions for 30 years from 1931, when he last saw his patient Rowland H, until 1961 when he replied to a letter from Bill Wilson,

The Deceptive Power of Masterly Inactivity

As mentioned, on their last meeting in 1931, after nearly a year of many therapy sessions, Carl Jung informed his patient Rowland H. of the 'hopelessness' as far as medical or psychiatric treatment was concerned in treating addiction to alcohol. This belated conclusion must have been devastating for a man who had spent a year living in Europe away from his home in America to have therapy to cure his addiction.

Bluntly, Jung said he could not help Roland H and wrote him off being helped by psychology. He made Roland H even more conscious of his powerlessness over his addiction. However, he said there might be hope for him if he became the subject of a religious experience or if he placed himself in the walls of a human community.

At first it seems that in 1931 Carl Jung was the first modern doctor to realise that medicine does not work for curing addictions. However, Temperance groups in the USA had known about this since the formation of the Washington

Temperance Society (The Washingtonians) in the Chase's Tavern in Baltimore in 1840. Jung had visited America in December 1924 and it is highly unlikely he would not have known about the Washingtonians, all the more because Abraham Lincoln had been a supporter of the Washingtonians.

Jung's advice to Roland H in 1931 was insightful and appeared ground-breaking. But did Jung derive the concept of mutual aid recovery from the American Washingtonians whom he would almost certainly have heard of during his visit to America in 1924?

When Rowland H returned to America he helped a fellow American, Bill Wilson, to recover from his alcoholism and in 1935 Wilson along with Dr Robert Smith went on to co-found Alcoholics Anonymous (AA).

In 1961, just months before Jung's death, Wilson wrote to thank Jung for his help in curing him of his addiction and his influence in helping to set up the first addiction recovery programme. Bill Wilson said Jung's conversation with Rowland H, his humility and deep perception played a critical role in the founding of the AA Fellowship.

'First of all, you frankly told him of his hopelessness, so far as any further medical or psychiatric treatment might be concerned. This candid and humble statement of yours was beyond doubt the first foundation stone upon which our Society has since been built.'

The two letters are reproduced on the link:
(See: https://silkworth.net/alcoholics-anonymous/dr-carl-jungs-letter-to-bill-w-jan-30-1961/).

Kusnacht-Zurich
Seestrasse 228

January 30, 1961

Mr. William G. Wilson
Alcoholics Anonymous
Box 459 Grand Central Station
New York 17, N.Y.

Dear Mr. Wilson,
Your letter has been very welcome indeed.

I had no news from Roland H. anymore and often wondered what has been his fate. Our conversation which he had adequately reported to you had an aspect of which he did not know. The reason, that I could not tell him everything, was that those days I had to be exceedingly careful of what I said. I had found out that I was misunderstood in every possible way. Thus I was very careful when I talked to Roland H. But what I really thought about, was the result of many experiences with men of his kind.

His craving for alcohol was the equivalent on a low level of the spiritual thirst of our being for wholeness, expressed in medieval language: the union with God. 1)

How could one formulate such an insight in a language that is not misunderstood in our days?

The only right and legitimate way to such an experience is, that it happens to you in reality and it can only happen to you when you walk on a path, which leads you to a higher understanding. You might be led to that goal by an act of grace or through a personal and honest contact with friends, or through a higher education of the mind beyond the confines of mere rationalism. I see from your letter that Roland H. has chosen the second way, which was, under the circumstances, obviously the best one.

I am strongly convinced that the evil principle prevailing in this world, leads the unrecognized spiritual need into perdition, if it is not counteracted either by a real religious insight or by the protective wall of human community. An ordinary man, not protected by an action from above and isolated in society cannot resist the power of evil, which is called very aptly the Devil. But the use of such words arouse so many mistakes that one can only keep aloof from them as much as possible.

These are the reasons why I could not give a full and sufficient explanation to Roland H. but I am risking it with you because I conclude from your very decent and honest letter, that you have acquired a point of view above the misleading platitudes, one usually hears about alcoholism. You see, Alcohol in Latin is "spiritus" and you use the same word for the highest religious experience as well as for the most depraving poison. The helpful formula therefore is: spiritus contra spiritum.

Thanking you again for your kind letter.

I remain yours sincerely,

C.G. Jung

1) "As the hart panteth after the water brooks, so Panteth my soul after thee, O God." (Psalm 42, 1)

Jung's immediate reply informed Bill Wilson that he had taken a risk at the time in advising Roland H that the only hope left for him was to lead a spiritually based life in a community. He said he could not have risked at that time telling Rowland H more in case he was misunderstood. This is worth looking at in more detail later.

As we have already seen, in this letter which Jung wrote shortly before he died, for the first time he acknowledged the importance of spirituality in recovery from addictions. Jung had thirty years of unique opportunities to show this new helpful spiritual path to the world but as he said in the letter he deliberately chose not to.

In this letter Jung wrote that he deliberately chose to conceal this to avoid being misunderstood. But was his motivation for not supporting Alcoholics Anonymous, the new increasingly popular mutual aid self help group, due in part to their potential for eclipsing and overshadowing his own intellectual theories.

He may have also concealed his knowledge of what the Roman Emperor Marcus Aurelius (120-180 CE) used to declare to his soldiers with the words:

'Espiritum vinci espiritus.'

(A rough translation of which is 'The spirit is conquered by the spirit')

In his reply to Bill Wilson Jung said that the words for the highest religious experience and alcohol are the same but he did not acknowledge the words 'Espiritum vinci espiritus,' which Marcus Aurelius used to declare to his soldiers.

Instead, Jung chose to paraphrase Marcus Aurelius's quote when he wrote to Bill Wilson when he said:

'The helpful formula therefore is . . .

"Spiritus contra spiritum."'

Jung also did not make this information available to doctors, to psychiatrists or to the public. Jung may have linked the two words together himself or more likely, unknowingly, he was quoting Marcus Aurelius. In which case he may have been displaying a condition which he wrote about, cryptomnesia, (hidden memory) which is when someone mistakenly believes that a current thought or idea is their creation when, in fact, they have forgotten they encountered it previously.

Carl Jung wrote about cryptomnesia in '*On the Psychology and Pathology of So-Called Occult Phenomena*' (1902) but it was first described by Théodore Flournoy, a Swiss professor of psychology who was a contemporary of Jung's.

With Jung's intelligence and almost encyclopaedic knowledge of ancient mythology and classical literature it is difficult to see why he did not directly quote Marcus Aurelius. Perhaps he chose not to in order to claim the privileged knowledge and wisdom as his own. This was possibly yet another incident of plagiarism.

Jung's Re-discovery and Concealment of a Cure

Unfortunately, it seems that it is almost impossible to praise Jung without in the same breath criticising him. This is not meant in a negative way about him. It is just that otherwise it would be taking a one sided view supporting Jung without mentioning the actual origins of what he said or his motivation and intentions.

Jung can be congratulated for eventually admitting at the last minute that psychiatrists, psychologists and therapists cannot help addicts. However, this could also be seen as Jung having deprived addicts of treatment and help he knew was useful from 1935 until 1961 which today would be seen as deeply unethical.

In his letter to Bill Wilson, Jung does not acknowledge withholding the treatment available through Alcoholics Anonymous. This is despite him knowing it was vital, as it could offer the only chance of a cure for many individuals. In an inescapable position he uses the rather lame and selfish excuse that he did not share the vital information about
mutual aid groups in case he was misunderstood.

Although in 1931 it would have been unusual for a medical doctor and psychiatrist to suggest a spiritual cure for addiction, it would not have been unusual coming from someone like Jung who was known for being unusual. On its own the possibility of being misunderstood is an insufficient explanation. He was wrong not to have mentioned it and supported rolling it out as effective cure for addictions until thirty years later in 1961.

During all of this time, when his reputation was not at risk, Jung would have been acutely aware of the success of Alcoholics Anonymous but he withheld his support for it until just before he died.

By then Alcoholics Anonymous was so well known to work for many people that Jung could have even seen one of the last ships of his earlier successful insights leaving without him on board. Perhaps he couldn't help himself supporting Alcoholics Anonymous at this late hour as he may have seen it as one of his last chances of being acknowledged. He was concerned with his legacy.

Drawing attention now to Jung's concealment of the two spiritual paths, 'Mutual Aid Groups' and 'Ramana Maharshi's path of Self-enquiry' is a belated way of compensating for the damage Jung did to them both as well as to doctors, therapists and Gurus in their ability to fully discharge this knowledge and wisdom during his lifetime and since then.

The Vital Importance of 12 Step Mutual Aid Groups

My reason for repeatedly emphasising the importance of mutual aid groups is because they are probably the most effective treatment for the most lethal, the most damaging and the most common psychological disorders such as eating disorders, drug addiction, alcohol addiction and gambling addiction.

I think it is largely because of Jung's lack of public support for mutual aid programmes from 1935 until 1961 that they were frequently not recognised and recommended as helpful to their patients by psychiatrists, psychologists and psychotherapists as they could have been.

Many people suffer unnecessarily longer at the hands of doctors and therapists when they might get better help and recover if they went to mutual aid groups such as Eating Disorders Anonymous, Sex Addiction Anonymous, Gamblers Anonymous, Narcotics Anonymous, Marijuana Anonymous, Alcoholics Anonymous and Al-Anon. But perhaps this could also be because doctors and therapists run businesses, have interests in keeping patients on their books or maybe because they just do not know about the help that can be obtained from mutual aid groups. Or like Jung they feel reluctant to invoke a higher spiritual authority for fear of being "misunderstood."

Once an addiction is identified in a consultation, there should be no hesitation in strongly recommending the patient to try 12 Step mutual aid meetings. Of course, they might need medical or other psychological help as well.

But it is pointless to be direct patients to be admitted to hospital and then afterwards to require them to attend 12 step mutual aid groups for life in order to stay 'clean.' Who benefits from this delay? . . .

It is like paying a year's salary to Rehab to find out that Alcoholics Anonymous or Narcotics Anonymous are free. Perhaps this delay could also be because help has been monetised. Rehab centres, Doctors and therapists run businesses, so they have interests in keeping patients on their books. Or maybe they just do not know about the help that can be obtained from mutual aid groups.

Doctors and psychiatrists still have the authority and power to suggest treatments for unhappiness. Many of which do not work and only "sedate" people enough for them to be socially more acceptable in their community. Doctors and psychiatrists also have the knowledge and skills to guide individuals to 12-Step mutual aid groups or to individual one-to-one therapy. They need to do this a lot more.

Therapists are trained to understand and help with our personal development usually by understanding and unblocking events where we have experienced pain and suffering. Therapists have usually become therapists because they have suffered a great deal. Because of their own healing and recovery many therapists eventually see that a spiritual path is the final path to true happiness. It is therefore no surprise that they may occasionally recommend a form of spiritual path for some individuals.

If a therapist identifies an addiction and carries on treating the addict without strongly suggesting they try mutual aid 12 step meetings, they are not putting the patients' interests first because substance abuses are more prone to harm in therapy.

Therapists perform a particularly difficult task and do it with good results but it is estimated that approximately 3-10% of patients become worse after psychotherapy, with higher rates of 7-15% for patients with 'substance abuse.'

(This was reported by N. Shpancer. When Talking Doesn't Cure: Negative Outcomes in Therapy. Psychology Today, March 2020) [1]

Gurus are concerned with helping us to recognise our ignorance about what we think we know. It is a path of unlearning. Nothing new can be added only the false removed. Gurus simply show us how to remove the darkness (our ignorance about ourselves) so we can see the light that is always here, like removing clouds from in front of the sun.

Just as it is vital to be aware of a doctor's, a therapist's and a guru's experience, we should not underestimate the importance of what is inside us, our own power to heal and be happy in ourselves. There have been many reminders.

"Everything in moderation" and *"Know thyself"*

On the portals of the temple of Delphi

"This above all-to thine own self be true, and it must follow as the night the day thou canst not be false to any man."

William Shakespeare
(Hamlet Act I Scene III)

"Happiness is your nature. It is not wrong to desire it. What is wrong is seeking it outside when it is inside."

'Your duty is to be: and not to be this or that. "I AM that I AM" sums up the whole truth. The method is summed up in the words *"BE STILL".* [2] [3]

Ramana Maharshi

10.

We are not born Unhappy

'Being on the path is also the goal'

10.

We are not born Unhappy

'We are not born unhappy.
When external circumstances make us unhappy
We can only find happiness within'

Our parents usually influence us more than anyone else in our lives. This was certainly the case for me. My mother was a Catholic western European from the west of Ireland whilst my father was an atheist Eastern European from eastern Ukraine. This was the backdrop of my changing from a western spiritual path to an eastern one.

I remember a fire and I remember being engulfed in it when I was just over two years old. It had happened on December 24th when there had been an accident in my parent's house. When I left hospital about six weeks later, I had woken up. This sense of being awake and conscious very slowly became clearer and clearer until I was about eleven.

The summer of 1967, which, for many, was the summer of love, saw the end of my innocence and the appearance for the first time of acute and painful sadness in my heart. I was 11 years old. It was Saturday night, and my 14 year old brother hadn't come home from playing cricket for his school. By six thirty, the school told my parents that he hadn't shown up for the cricket match.

At seven o'clock, they phoned the police who searched the whole house including the attic where we used to play. We did not know if he was hiding, if he had run away, if he

111

had been abducted or if he was dead. By the end of the first week, Interpol had been contacted, and there was a picture of my brother in the local papers and on the local TV stations.

At eleven, the sudden disappearance of my 14 year old brother created a catastrophic family crisis which increased over one and a half years. My parents were distraught and I received no support from school. However, because of the stress at home, I was made exempt from being caned at school for my errors.

My brother's running away from home for nearly two years left me in shock at his deception. I felt abandoned, alone and sad as I also quickly realised, I was isolated from my two sisters who were older and disinterested in their younger brother. I also witnessed and felt the acute then chronic sorrow, which my parents were experiencing at the loss of their son.

At school, no one said anything to me about my missing brother as if it was taboo or they just didn't know. The local priest sought solace in alcohol like my war traumatised father so there was no one to go to for support, hope and understanding. These days my father would be diagnosed with Complex Post Traumatic Stress Disorder (PTSD) which was not described until 1980.

Although I didn't wallow in the feelings I was experiencing, I was acutely aware that I was without any help or understanding of what was going on inside me. The pain was like a gnawing hunger for help. Meanwhile I was expected to respond and tried to respond to all of the people in my world normally whilst inside I was confused and unsupported because my family was broken. I wrote letters to my grandmother in Ireland and I tried listening to my radio under the blankets at night to produce a happier inner life but my life remained the same.

I knew I was in a difficult situation but I didn't just accept this and continued to look for a solution. For weeks I searched in books. Then I began to find myself in the middle of a book by a nun called Theresa of Lisieux, *The Story of a Soul* and for the first time I felt like I was listening to a fellow child speaking.

However, the strange and attractive thing about her was that she was describing how she was so happy because of her suffering. I wondered how anyone could be so happy because of their suffering, whilst I was miserable. But what was even more mysterious was that she looked out for suffering and deliberately put herself through pain as a way to happiness.

I liked what she wrote about being like a simple wildflower in the forest subjected to the elements of nature but also nurtured by them so that she could flourish while Knowing all along that she was part of nature too.

"He opened the book of nature before me, and I saw that every flower He has created has a beauty of its own, that the splendour of the rose and the lily's whiteness do not deprive the violet of its scent nor make less ravishing the daisy's charm. I saw that if every little flower wished to be a rose, nature would lose her spring adornments, and the fields would be no longer enamelled with their varied flowers." [1]

I took her on as my reference point, my friend, who was also a saint. I also took her as someone I could speak to and who would listen to me unconditionally. I had internalised her as an ideal person as if she were not just a religious saint but more, perhaps even as an early Guru who had attained happiness, perfection whilst alive and who knew the answer to suffering.

This was successful because it helped me cope and worked for a few months. Then she faded away. What I had actively imagined her to be for me, helped me through an extremely difficult period of my childhood.

What she had done was to be an example of simplicity, gentleness. She was also an example of complete surrender and unconditional love.

There was honesty in St Theresa of Lisieux's trust and complete self-surrender. She practiced detachment of everything about herself to love what she saw as her sense of her soul, which she saw as God. The more she forgot about herself and deliberately suffered, the more she experienced a feeling of love in herself. Here was a shining example of acceptance. Of gratefulness. And the result was happiness. In my state, how could I not try and emulate her.

Towards the end of the book, I read that she wore a cross with sharp points on the back to produce physical pain. I had nothing to lose so I pushed four drawing pins through a cross I bought at the local church. I tried wearing it, pushing it against my chest, eventually stopping because it was too much. As an adult, I learnt that she had to give this up because it made her ill.

These days it could be seen as self-flagellation, self-harm or an ignorant attempt at an endorphin high. But I was actually just looking for happiness and love. With the family in a state of grave unhappiness, personal happiness and love was on hold and seemed impossible. So, at that time anything was worth a try to find some kind of love and happiness.

I was looking for understanding and for love. I knew they were there. I knew I could love, but whom? The easiest, most available target was God . . . not a Christian or Hindu god, or a god of any religion, but a sense of myself being one with something greater, almost as if I was superimposing an image on the stars in the sky. I realised that I was distilling my own sense of God. It was an act of transferring something from deep inside me, a sort of 'inner me', onto someone or something that was on the edge of my consciousness that I could not quite grasp.

Everything tangible that I had learnt or knew had turned out to be unreliable. I was trying to become self-reliant, not only on a worldly plane, but in my sense reality, my truth, of the spiritual. I sensed this was more dependable, permanent and more real, and had more meaning even though it couldn't be touched but only felt deep inside.

This revelation of the tangible being unreal and the intangible being real came to me through pain, and in the process of searching for happiness. I had turned inwards because I had not been able to find happiness anywhere outside. What began as a conscious projection of my inner Self onto the stars then took five years to turn into a meditative, sense of just being.

Most importantly, I saw her example and description of complete Self-surrender was the way to the soul, to the Self. She forgot about herself and turned her life over to her inner sense at every opportunity she could in all her encounters.

As much as I could see that happiness was not outside me, I had learnt that outward physical suffering was not necessary, only inner surrender. This was the first turning inwards. It was only then that my sense of pain, from the burden of my thinking, seemed to disappear. I experienced a unity of happiness about everything, in everything. I had a new lightness of my heart I had not known was possible. It was if I was intoxicated by happiness.

Five years later in 1972, perhaps my adolescence pulled me towards the east and once more inwards. At sixteen whilst I was on a school trip to the Hayward Gallery in London, I noticed an Indian friend of mine sitting very relaxed and still with his eyes closed. He looked like he was in a state which I had never seen before. What opened my eyes was that he was in a state of happiness and peace, and so I asked him what he was doing. He said he was meditating and had learnt it from a local teacher.

Mantras and Breathing

Within a week I had paid my instructor with money borrowed from my parents and was using a sound to bring my distracted mind back constantly to one thing, just the sound. It was my first experience of mind control. I learnt a mantra meditation which had become popular in the 1960s. Using a mantra, I was able to move inside close to the place where I had previously found such blissful happiness when I was 11 years old.

This mantra or japa meditation is simple inner repetition of a sound and is found in most eastern religions such as Hinduism, Jainism, Sikhism, Buddhism, and Shintoism.

But there was something not quite right about this which I found difficult to be precise about. I had an awkward sense, almost artificialness about the mantra technique, as if I had the wrong clothes on. I had paid money for a popular relaxation technique, which was later virtually replaced by mindfulness.

As a teenager, I learnt that a spiritual path could not be paid for with money. The only currency of exchange for learning spirituality is complete surrender of the ego.

I had a varying relationship with mantra/japa meditation. It came and went quickly as something I did to tether my mind whenever I found it difficult to focus and settle my mind because of outside disturbance.

I gave it up soon after I learnt it because although it had helped me re-discover my inner peace, I realised it could take me no further.

I saw it was a vehicle to be used only to get across a river, not a ferry you live on forever. It was not entirely without merit, but the way it was being sold, as if it was more than a ferry was deception and overselling. Some people do mantra/japa meditation only and find that this is what they are happy with. I am happy for them and in what it gives them. But one size does not suit all and I was a misfit.

I found the explanation of how this type of meditation worked too simple because it lacked more in-depth explanation. There was no adequate traceable history of its origins which troubled me.

It seemed to me at the time that there was also something uncomfortably wrong about paying for it. This bothered me and I wondered just how you can buy spirituality? Something didn't fit.

After some inner searching, I saw that just having a means such as the 'method' of using a mantra or a breathing technique to attain inner stillness is not enough. Inner stillness with its silencing of thoughts is not enough. There has to be meaning because meditation on its own is without meaning. When stillness becomes aware of its meaning, this is our meaning, our own truth. This is common to all, only veiled by thoughts.

Instead of continuing with the method mantra/japa meditation, I stopped and began reading about people who were regarded as experts who taught meditation. At first no one grabbed my attention. I read about gurus but this was the 1970s and 1980s when gurus had a questionable reputation.

The method Ramana Maharshi advocated was simply 'being still.' He said a mantra or breathing method could be used for those who had difficulty but was not essential and added that he never used either.

He was asked by Prof D. S. Sarma if he had a period of Sadhana (daily spiritual practice) in his life.

M.: 'I know of no such period. I never performed any Pranayama or Japa (method of breath control or a mantra). I know no mantras. I had no rules of meditation or contemplation. Even when I came to hear of such things later, I was never attracted by them. Even now my mind refuses to pay any attention to them. Sadhana implies an object to be gained and the means of gaining it. What is there to be gained which we do not already possess? In meditation, concentration and contemplation, what we have to do is only, not to think of anything but to be still. Then we shall be in our natural state . . . the Self is realised not by one's doing something, but by one's refraining from doing anything by remaining still and being simply what one really is.' [2]

The ingredient he had which was lacking in my mantra meditation was 'meaning' which he simply called 'truth' and this was eventually reached by asking the question, 'Who am I?'

He summarised the 'truth' and the 'method' simply by saying:

'Your duty is to be: and not to be this or that. "I AM that I AM" [3] sums up the whole truth. The method is summed up in "BE STILL". [4]

Perhaps the formula is: *Stillness + Meaning = Happiness*

He suggested enquiring into what our personal thinking consisted of. He said that if this was done diligently by going to the root of thought that our ignorance would be removed and we would see that the ego is only a collection of thoughts.

119

He put it differently to anyone else:

"The removal of ignorance is the aim of practice and not the acquisition of Realisation." [5]

Surprisingly, he also advised that total surrender could produce exactly the same result. He said:

"It is enough that one surrenders oneself. Surrender is to give oneself up to the original cause of ones being. Do not delude yourself by imagining such source to be some God outside you. One's source is within oneself. Give yourself up to it. That means that you should see the source and merge in it." [6]

It was only after some considerable time following Ramana Maharshi's advice that I could see that St Theresa of Lisieux and Ramana Maharshi led almost exactly the same lives. It was one of always turning inwards. They were both consumed by their surrender. Journeys in different directions for truth have but one destination. A person's circumstances may be different but the inner means and destination are the same.

There are other striking parallels. They are both widely regarded as saints in their own countries. St Theresa of Lisieux was born in France in 1873 and Ramana Maharshi in South India in 1879. Her mother died when she was four years old whilst his father died when he was 13 years old. St Theresa of Lisieux entered a Carmelite convent aged 15 and stayed there until her death aged 24 from tuberculosis. Ramana Maharshi left home aged 16 and lived a life of silence on the mountain Arunachala until he died aged 70 from a sarcoma on his upper arm.

St Theresa of Lisieux lived a hidden life in a Carmelite convent and wanted to be unknown but she became famous after her spiritual autobiography "The Story of a Soul." Ramana Maharshi lived on Arunachala; virtually sitting still in silence for 54 years.

They both led lives of complete surrender, having given up who they previously were and dedicating their lives to spiritual practice. It seems as if neither tried to avoid any suffering, which they encountered because they were already consumed. There are no recordings of their voices but there are written records of some of their words. They both wrote little.

Their early lives were characterised by profound loss, which must have been unbearably painful. Whilst barely out of childhood they both renounced the material world and entered the environment where they would spend the rest of their lives.

Curiously, St Theresa of Lisieux was surrounded by her blood sisters in the convent and Ramana Maharshi was surrounded by his mother and brother on Arunachala. It seems like once in the convent and on Arunachala their worldly achievements came to an end as outwardly, they appeared to do nothing more. Nevertheless, this was just the beginning of their work.

Their complete surrender of permanently retreating into the inner world and not identifying with the personal ego continue to shine out brilliantly as rare examples of living fully in the spiritual domain. They lived in two different cultures influenced by two different religions but their inner means and destination unified their different paths.

The result was happiness in the form of bliss.

There is not much more to add to this, which is helpful. You have to see what they were able to be. You have to want it. Then you have to get on with it in your own way, wherever you are.

The catastrophic family crisis triggered by my brother's running away and total disappearance for eighteen months created an opportunity for me. It showed me a path, turning me inwards and unveiling my inner happiness.

Although this inner path may not always seem easy for us to access, it is here now and there is always help. Ramana Maharshi and St Theresa of Lisieux are like two silent guiding beacons, lighting up the path for us.

11.

Pushed from Outside
and
Pulled from Inside

'When inside and outside merge, there is no inside or outside'

11.

Pushed from Outside and Pulled from Inside

'Awareness of the unity of no subject or object is realisation'

My own experience has changed how I see myself being one with everything, with the Multiverse. My inner stillness is still my default, my refuge, my Self.

I return to stillness more frequently and more automatically just to find myself in stillness. Staying on my path still takes effort and can be a fight, so once or twice every day I have to start from scratch.

Let me give you an example of my experience during a fairly typical day . . .

It's four twenty in the morning and I've woken two hours before I wanted to. It is still dark and cold.

I lie here and I do not move. I know I won't be able to sleep any more. But I do not move. I wait and watch my thoughts rising, churning, keeping my consciousness occupied.

I know this will continue if I do not do something to stop my thoughts.

I get up out of bed and go and sit in a chair. I light some incense to remind me that I am doing something which is subtle and nothing to do with thoughts.

I look at the clock to see what time I start.

I close my eyes and ask Who am I? I know this is stepping on to the path to unveil my happiness.

At first my answer to the question Who am I? takes me to memories of my experiences, but these are the past. The next answer is desires I have, but these are the future.

Having no answer to the question Who am I? leads to the next question, What am I? and I know I am the witness asking this, so what is this witness? The only answer to this is, the witness is awareness.

So, I ask what is this awareness? My answer is awareness is being aware that I am awareness. There are no words for it, so I see it as my 'I am-ness.' I concentrate on experiencing just being awareness. 'The experience of 'I am awareness' or 'I am' is the only thing I know is definitely me.

The only awareness I have is of right now. Any attempt to be anything else is a thought about awareness, and not awareness itself, only thoughts about it. Meditation seems to come to a gentle end.

My awareness is Self aware. It is Self awareness. It is not just an individual isolated consciousness. It is part of the consciousness that is everyone. Maybe we believe animals don't have it because they do not have the means of language to communicate it to us. Perhaps it is the intangible 'stuff' of the Universe, the Multiverse, the great unifier.

Being dissatisfied and rudderless as a student in London in 1974, I started looking for something else and so once again I looked in books but my search was unfruitful. In the summer of 1982, I was at a week of talks given by Jiddu Krishnamurti at Brockwood Park.

After the talk he wandered over to where I was standing. I remember I was standing about two feet from him and I had a strange intuition. He was talking to someone and I realised although my mind liked the eloquent talk he had just given, I somehow felt uncomfortable and knew he was definitely not right for me and I simply walked away.

I knew he was able to give eloquent talks which attracted people's minds. My mind did not need any more eloquent sentences strung together to stimulate it. My mind needed to get into neutral and have no thoughts. To me he did not seem able to give this message of how to have inner stillness. He was elegant like royalty but he had nothing to give me or that I could receive.

I had given two young men a couple of years older than me a lift to Brockwood park in my car. They had both been to a sacred mountain in South India. They spoke of people going on pilgrimages there and of a Silent Guru who had lived there, who had died in 1950.

When I asked what he taught, the answer seemed vague to me. It seemed he didn't say much but sat in silence nearly all the time. He taught through silence. A written record of over four years, showed he didn't speak on sixty percent of the days. When he did speak it was only about a hundred and fifty words.

I remember having difficulty pronouncing his name, the name of the mountain he lived on and the town it was in.

His name was Ramana Maharshi. He lived on the mountain called Arunachala in the small town of Tiruvannamalai in the Southern state of Tamil Nadu.

For some unknown reason, or perhaps lack of reasoning, this interested me. I didn't understand this and so I was intrigued. How could someone who didn't say anything teach meditation?

However, it was not until 1985 that I eventually I came to Arthur Osborne's book *Ramana Maharshi and the Path of Self Knowledge* [1] and I realised from this that the search for me was simply one of always turning inwards.

I decided that I needed to go to India and see if Arunachala was as special as I had heard and read about.

When I started reading about Ramana Maharshi, I discovered that he didn't make any claim to teach meditation. This intrigued me even more and I needed to find an explanation for this myself. I also noticed that I heard his name mentioned more often than I had previously.

A few months later, I visited the mountain in South India where this Silent Guru lived most of his life.

After a gruelling but interesting five-hour bus journey from Madras, I got to my destination - Arunachala. I arrived at Arunachala with only the clothes I stood in.

It was early winter in England, but a steamy thirty degrees in South India and my summer clothes were with the rest of my luggage, which the airline had sent back to England and then lost.

It was the 1985 and Tiruvannamalai was quiet with only a handful of visitors at the Ashram.

What struck me most at first was the immediate feeling of inner peace in the Old Hall, which I visited twice a day. Although I stayed in a cave on Arunachala for some nights, amidst the hustle and bustle of Tiruvannamalai, I failed to notice the most important aspect of Arunachala.

My visit was not just an introduction to the place and the people, it raised the question, 'What are all these people doing here around this mountain?' Some said they were only there because the mountain attracted them. Some said they were devotees of one guru or another, but most said they were there only because of the Silent Guru.

I couldn't work it out. I was also distracted by the smells, the colours, the food, the people and the hustle and bustle of India. I found it difficult to focus my mind on one thing. I couldn't even meditate there.

When I visited, I initially saw what looked and felt to me like a mausoleum. There was a large structure built over the Silent Guru's tomb. There was a dining space, an office and some basic rooms to stay in. This was where he had lived and taught by sitting in silence for decades.

What I saw with my eyes was an old graveyard which had been built on and later became an ashram. Since the Silent Guru's death it now seemed to me like a mausoleum. However, my intuition told me that there was something here but I just couldn't see it. I could strongly sense it but not see it or work it out. There was a simple reason for this. I was looking at the wrong landscape, the landscape of the outer world. I couldn't see the inner land inside me because I didn't know how to look inside. Because I didn't understand this, and knew I didn't, I said goodbye to the place and returned to England exhausted.

∞

A year later, I was back, even though I was unable to say why.

Nothing I read seemed to give me an understanding of the Silent Guru. I couldn't come up with words to explain this place, the mountain of the Silent Guru. I walked around the mountain. I spoke to people who lived there.

I left feeling something was beginning to happen to me, but I wasn't t sure what. I couldn't put any words to it. It was intangible, subtle and there was no questioning of what it was.

I knew something in me was ever so slowly unfolding. It seemed to me that whatever was happening inside me, there was nothing I could do to find out about it, change it or speed it up.

My outer life carried on as did whatever was happening inside me. I had given up trying to control what was happening inside me. Instead, I listened. I waited.

I waited until I was not able to resist some kind of strange yearning inside me which I felt compelled to listen to and do whatever it said. I knew it was the neediest part of me which trumped any importance of my daily work.

Another year passed and I still didn't know why I was once more back at the foot of this mountain living in a simple rented room, which was a thatched mud hut. I had travelled thousands of miles again and again and I was angry at myself for not being able to work it out. But I was also totally intrigued by what was going on in my inner self which I had no control over. Once again, I sensed that something was happening inside me which I couldn't work out, but now it was getting stronger.

To me, in photographs, the Silent Guru had a compassionate face. It seemed as if he could see me. I thought maybe I was trying to see in myself what he seemed to be able to see in me. Was it his photograph that was slowly turning me inwards or was I turning inwards because I wanted to and needed to. I know with certainty now that I was being pushed and pulled.

I had started looking in a different direction. Turning inwards made me feel strangely good and more detached from people and the world outside. Was it really his compassionate look in his photograph that was turning me inwards? If it was, then it was so subtle. If it was, then no words were involved. If it was, then words still cannot describe how it works.

I wasn't able to articulate this because I was trusting something inside me more than I was trusting things I could talk about.

And I still am.

What was this Silent Guru's compassionate look about? Was it just compassion? Was it that his eyes seemed as if they could see deep inside me? Was it a look of understanding? Was it a look of peace and tranquillity? I knew it wasn't only one of these. There was a look I understood inside me but could not name, no matter how much I tried. Is it love? Is it Grace? Words do not matter or change it.

I sensed something about him in me because somehow something was being uncovered inside me. I was identifying with something in him from his photograph. I have looked at many photographs and there is one which when I first saw it on the back of a book, sent a shiver up my spine as if this person was actually looking not just at me but deep inside me. I saw that it was me seeing inside me. When I look at this photograph I see an almost questioning look and also a reassuring look. It is as if he and I are saying in silence:

'You know you are you doing this because this is the right thing for you.'

There was no moment I can pinpoint but slowly I became conscious that there was something about the sight of the mountain which had an effect on me. I had a sense of calmness in me which I could identify with the mountain. Again, just like the Silent Guru's silence I could not put it into words. I began to understand that the silence of the guru, the effect of the mountain and what was happening in me, were all beyond words.

From what I read about the Silent Guru, I understood that most of the time he was silent. It took me some time to really understand what this silence was, what it reflected. His silence was not about not speaking. His silence was not about him not producing a sound and being quiet.

His silence came from the inner stillness that lies beyond thought. He had control over his mind so that thoughts didn't keep relentlessly appearing in his mind. This was because he was focused entirely on consciousness itself. He was able to be just consciousness. I repeat: his silence was inner stillness. It was the silence of not having thoughts.

The Path is the Goal

Experiencing simply being conscious of I AM is all we can attain. It is simple removal of ignorance. Staying with being conscious of this by experiencing 'being still' stops and eclipses thought. This lets us see that the path is none other than the goal.

This is what Ramana Maharshi communicated so eloquently about meditation and contemplation in his silent stillness and is summarised in answer to a question. He was asked by Prof D. S. Sarma if he had a period of Sadhana (daily spiritual practice) in his life. His answer to this is worth repeating because it is simple and subtle, containing the 'method' but it also explains the answer to the question 'Who am I?' which follows a long and arduous time before it is answered.

M.: 'I know of no such period. I never performed any Pranayama or Japa (methods of using breath control or a mantra). I know no mantras. I had no rules of meditation or contemplation. Even when I came to hear of such things later, I was never attracted by them. Even now my mind refuses to pay any attention to them. Sadhana implies an object to be gained and the means of gaining it. What is there to be gained which we do not already possess? In meditation, concentration and contemplation, what we have to do is only, not to think of anything but to be still. Then we shall be in our natural state . . . the Self is realised not by one's doing something, but by one's refraining from doing anything by remaining still and being simply what one really is.' [2]

The state of having no thoughts is having a still mind. Although a still mind can be achieved by mantra meditation, which is what I had experienced for short periods when I did mantra meditation, I had also experienced it when I read and followed St Theresa of Lisieux.

The Silent Guru said that the 'method' in his teaching was simply, 'Be Still' and that the truth was summed up in, 'I AM That I AM.'

For a long time, I didn't understand the relevance of Arunachala and especially what it meant to the Silent Guru. He always maintained that the mountain was his guru and the mountain was also God.

He went further and said that your Self, the Guru, the Mountain and God were all the same.

I couldn't understand this. How could they possibly all be the same? I felt lacking in perception of what was going on.

Eventually I understood the importance of the mountain to the Silent Guru. It is still. Its stillness reflects our inner stillness, the stillness of having no thoughts. To the Silent Guru, his own silence and stillness were the same at the stillness of the mountain.

I hadn't seen this when I stayed on the mountain during my early visits. Perhaps this is what had been pulling me back to the mountain.

The Silent Guru repeatedly said that to know 'the Self' and have happiness we should ask who we are. He suggested asking the question, 'Who am I?'

His answer to this question is Biblical and is worth repeating:

He quoted the Biblical statement of 'I Am That I Am.' When Moses asked God for his name he answered, 'I Am that I Am. Thus shalt you say unto the children of Israel, I Am has sent me to you.' Jehovah means I am. So, knowing the Self, God is known as they are taken to be the same.

The truth of this resonated with other Biblical sayings such as 'Be still and know that I am God.' [3] (Psalm 46) and 'The kingdom of God is within you.' (Luke 17:20-21) [4]

The Silent Guru was showing how to see the Self and how to see that it is also the supreme cosmic spirit. It doesn't matter what it is called, God or Brahman, or the Multiverse because most importantly the Silent Guru was showing us how to be still, how to be the Self without thoughts.

He said that when the mind becomes absorbed in the heart, by being the consciousness of 'I am,' the ego vanishes and only consciousness of the Self remains. This is what he called Silence.

With more constant being the consciousness of 'I am,' 'I am' becomes the default consciousness.

The outer world is now perceived as being one and the same as us, not separate. A oneness which may have only been occasionally glimpsed in meditation becomes the default way of being.

All I can tell you is I learnt this thanks to the Silent Guru. I cannot fully explain in words what he taught because it cannot be explained with words. It can only be experienced.

12.

Experiential Knowledge

'The more you know, the more you are in your grave. Knowing is not being'

Unknown

12.

Experiential Knowledge

I didn't start out trying to learn how to meditate or how to surrender to the inner Self. Suffering led me to these things only after it had brought me to my knees. After much searching, I realised happiness can only be found inside.

This search came with a clear warning which was also a formula:

"Arunachala! You will tear out by the roots the ego of those who meditate in their hearts saying, 'Arunachala.' " [1]

We can destroy our illusory ego by repeatedly defaulting to the Self in meditation. There are no thoughts. It works. When we do this from the heart, for long enough and often enough the default becomes more permanent. The deal is simple. The price we pay for our Self is our ego. This is the way happiness is unveiled.

Being still is having no thoughts. This can be achieved with repeated effort. It can also be achieved with the help of mantras or with the help of breath control.

Whichever way, it is a fight which goes on.

Being still sounds simple.

Much of the time the effort required to quieten the mind is a struggle.

Indeed, it can be a struggle which even resembles a fight. Much of the time it is a fight.

This is because we are conditioned to think all the time. Before thinking can be brought to a standstill, the mind needs to be tethered to a single thought. Otherwise, it spontaneously keeps on producing thoughts. Even when it is brought to a standstill for a few moments, it seems to relentlessly re-activate. This tendency is not as inevitable as it seems because it is only conditioning. It requires a lot of effort to overcome this conditioning which enables thoughts be the centre of our attention. But eventually the thoughts move more to the side.

Turning inside and asking,' Who am I?' is learning through experience. It is experiential learning because we learn by practising then reflecting on what took place. How we learn it is rather like learning to ride a bicycle, drive a car or sail a boat because it cannot be learnt through studying books or manuals, but only through practical experience.

There is no question of logical evidence for the answer to 'Who am I?' because it can only be confirmed by knowledge of personal experience, which is our observation of ourselves. The answer to the question, 'Who am I? is seen by our conscious intuition, and is verifiable only from knowledge of personal experience rather than by theory or logic.

Asking 'Who am I?' removes the false sense of who we are i.e., that we are a bundle of thoughts called the ego and then seeing we are the cosmic Self, 'That' which is everything. Seeing this, understanding this and being this is conscious intuition, only seen from certainty of empirical experiential knowledge.

We cannot be taught the answer to the question, 'Who am I?' because we can only find the answer by looking for it inside the Self. We do not need any other intermediary to show their answer to us and we do not need any interpretation. We need to find out about the Self on our own without teachers.

Having any followers of any kind does not help us to find out about our Self. Flattery clouds our consciousness by inflating our ego, which is the reverse of our aim. What we need to do is to do nothing, only be still.

Having a lineage of any kind implies a hierarchy, something which is only needed in an organised institution to denote lines of authority.

The vital importance of the independence of 'our own' search for truth is illustrated simply in an aphorism of which only the first half is usually remembered. The author is unknown:

'When the student is ready the teacher will appear.

When the student is truly ready . . . The teacher will disappear'

∞

141

Appendix

Curiously, Jung is very dismissive of Ramana Maharshi in his letter to Dr Mees. Like Zimmer, Dr Mees strongly encouraged Jung to visit Ramana Maharshi but was probably left surprised and disappointed by Jung's avoidant behaviour. In his letter to Mees, Jung perhaps misleadingly, refers to Ramana Pillai, who wasn't a disciple of Ramana Maharshi.

"I'm sorry that I was under the impression when we met in Trivandrum that you introduced your friend Raman Pillai as a remote pupil of Sri Ramana. This however doesn't matter very much, since the basic coincidence of most of the Indian teaching is so overwhelmingly great that it means little whether the author is called Ramakrishna or Vivekananda or Sri Aurobindo, etc." [1]   See: https://carljungdepthpsychologysite.blog/2020/04/12/ramana/

It is very uncharacteristic of Jung to get such an important detail wrong but what is worse is that he doesn't seem to care and just rationalises it by a sweeping generalisation.

Jung not only generalises, which reveals his lack of understanding of the subtleties of Indian spirituality, he repeatedly uses the excuse that Ramana Maharshi was just the same as any other Indian teacher to explain why he avoided meeting him.

"For the fact is, I doubt his uniqueness; he is of a type which always was and will be. Therefore, it was not necessary to seek him out. I saw him all over India, in the pictures of Ramakrishna, in Ramakrishna's disciples, . . ."

In the same paragraph Jung carries on describing Ramana Maharshi but it is as if he is talking about a different person.

"Sri Ramana Maharshi is a true son of the Indian Earth. He is "genuine," and on top of that he is a "phenomenon," which seen through European eyes, has claims to uniqueness. But in India he is merely the whitest spot on a white surface." [2]

Jung justifies his decision not to meet Ramana Maharshi by saying that Ramana Pillai had surpassed Ramana Maharshi and that nothing better could have happened to Jung by meeting him. [3] In his letter to Dr Mees, Jung seems not to know much, if anything, about Ramana Maharshi's teachings and points out that by the time he got to Madras, he didn't care anymore to meet anyone like him. [4]

In evaluating this sharp retort of Jung's, one can make the argument that after the energetic tour of north India, which had profoundly affected him, along with his recent illness, Jung was so overloaded with intense impressions that he could not absorb more for fear of jeopardising his hard-won balance. He was in a state of rebellion and retreated into an intense study of western alchemy fuelled by the insights he had gained during the trip.

Jung's wonder at who Ramana Maharshi was in 'The Holy Men of India' is essential in attempting to understand Jung's ambivalent comments because it is the only time Jung openly admits he doesn't understand Ramana Maharshi at all. This is compelling evidence to prove that Jung's approach to 'the Self' was purely intellectual and inadequate.

Jung's hazy intellectual understanding of Ramana

Maharshi's immersion in the Self is significant because Jung was almost certainly misguided by fear of another mental breakdown. The fundamental Eastern realisation is that the atman, 'the Self' is Sat Chit Ananda (Being - Consciousness - Bliss) and can only be understood by practical experience.

Yet Jung talks about realisation of the Self as someone who describes what a plane looks like and what it does but has never flown one himself and therefore cannot give any advice on how to fly it.

It appears that he could not afford the risk of directly attempting to realise 'the Self' in the sense of Being-Consciousness-Bliss for fear of a relapse into his previous psychotic illness as happened after his traumatic split with Freud.

Paul Brunton's Interfering Influence on Jung

Although Paul Brunton enthusiastically praised Ramana Maharshi in his 1934 book *A Search in Secret India* [5] which had a major impact on many readers, Brunton may well also have had a strong influence in persuading Jung not to visit Ramana Maharshi.

In the period between 1934 and when Jung visited India in 1937, Brunton had fallen out with Ramana Maharshi's ashram, probably due to a serious disagreement with Swami Niranjanananda, the younger brother of Ramana Maharshi and administrator of the ashram. In *Talks with Sri Ramana Maharshi*, Ramana Maharshi was asked about someone who had clearly made unfavourable comments about either himself or the ashram. Brunton had been at Sri Ramanasramam earlier in 1936.

"27th September 1936. A certain devotee asked about some disagreeable statements made by a certain man well known to Maharshi.

"He said, 'I permit him to do so. I have permitted him already. Let him do so even more. Let others follow suit. Only let them leave me alone. If because of these reports no one comes to me, I shall consider it a great service done to me. Moreover, if he cares to publish books containing scandals of me, and if he makes money by their sale, it is really good. Such books will sell even more quickly and in larger numbers than the others. Look at Miss Mayo's book. Why should he not also do it? He is doing me a very good turn.' Saying so, he laughed." [6]   Ramana Maharshi was unaffected by the negative publicity.

In another of his books *The Hidden Teaching beyond Yoga*, which was published in 1941; Brunton complains that he didn't get the guidance he wanted from Ramana Maharshi. He also seems very disgruntled with everything to do with Ramana Maharshi and Sri Ramanasramam.

"But during my last two visits to India it had become painfully evident that the institution known as the Ashram which had grown around him during the past few years, and over which his ascetic indifference to the world rendered him temperamentally disinclined to exercise the slightest control, could only greatly hinder and not help my own struggles to attain the highest goal, so I had no alternative but to bid it an abrupt and final farewell." [7]
However, there was a major shift in his perceptions earlier

145

in 1936 when he returned to Sri Ramanasramam and it seems that he was the one who made the disagreeable statements which Ramana Maharshi found so amusing. We can only guess what his gripe was. Jeffery Masson describes how Brunton spoke with Indian journalists about Ramana Maharshi in his book *My Father's Guru*:

"What exactly happened between P.B., the Maharshi and the Maharshi's brother is not known. But whatever it was-evidently P.B. gave interviews in the Indian papers that the brother did not find satisfactory-it soured the relationship between all three men." [8]

If it was Brunton who made the disagreeable statements in 1936, after terminating his relationship with Ramana Maharshi, Brunton may well also have discouraged Jung from visiting him. This seems likely as Jung met Brunton in 1937 along with Brunton's new guru V. Subrahmanya Iyer.

But instead of Jung meeting Ramana Maharshi when he visited India as he was encouraged to do by Heinrich Zimmer, Jung visited Brunton's new guru, Iyer who was also the guru of the Maharajah of Mysore. After returning from India Jung continued to write to Iyer who had a similar intellectual approach which Jung probably favoured over the apparently simple but subtle, direct approach of Ramana Maharshi.

Paul Brunton is another guru whom Storr describes in his book *Feet of Clay*. If Brunton's abandonment of Ramana Maharshi was the main cause of Jung not meeting Ramana Maharshi it is worthwhile investigating what kind of person he was. Brunton's real name was Raphael Hurst and Storr describes him as follows:

"Brunton exhibited many of the traits and forms of behaviour characteristic of gurus. He was secretive about his origins and revealed nothing of his personal life in any of his books. If one claims, as he did to have had many previous lives and to have come to earth from another planet, the less that is known about what the actual circumstances of one's birth and childhood the better. Brunton's claim to wisdom largely rested upon memories derived from his previous incarnations and upon his assertion that higher beings residing in other parts of the universe had passed on their esoteric knowledge to him." [9]

Uncharacteristically, for such an eminent psychiatrist and psychotherapist, Storr shows an astonishing deliberate lack of interest in the circumstances of Brunton's birth and also his childhood. Essentially, Storr is implying that there are some things best left unsaid. One of the characteristics of gurus with feet of clay is that they are often confidence tricksters. He does however examine Brunton's thinking.

"Although Brunton narcissistically claimed that he was particularly spiritually advanced, and that he possessed an aura of such strength that it protected him against evil assaults, he was also frightened of insanity. However, his paranoid delusions of persecution served to explain how it was that such a gifted and important person had not been even more successful, and thus preserved his self-esteem." [10]

Jeffery Masson was much more critical than Storr of Brunton's unjustified claims. For example Brunton claimed to know Sanskrit. Masson not only had a PhD in Sanskrit from Harvard but he was also professor of Sanskrit

147

at the University of Toronto. Brunton lived in his parent's household for some considerable time.

"The more I learned about India, the more I realized how little P.B actually knew. This began to enrage me. I felt I had been taken in, duped. It was all a trick. P.B knew no Sanskrit, knew no texts, invented things, lied, cheated and stole, intellectually speaking. How could I have been so stupid? In spirit, P.B might have been like the Indian sages he idolized. His ideas may have been similar to theirs. But he did not really represent any tradition, any body of knowledge, any other person - in fact anything at all. He was just a hodgepodge of misread and misunderstood ideas from an ancient culture he did not know or understand. In this sense he was a phony, a charlatan, a mountebank, an imposter, a quack. I couldn't find enough words to describe my disappointment." [11]

I would temper the above observations of an author who has coloured his memoir with the bitter animus of one whose childhood dreams were shattered when he realised his mentor had feet of clay. We need to view this disillusionment with some degree of equanimity.

In the closing words of his chapter on Brunton Storr once again shows fairmindedness and humane insight into Brunton' mental state.

"The diagnosis of mental illness should not be made on the evidence of beliefs alone; however eccentric they may appear. I have tried to demonstrate that a new belief system whether it is considered delusional or not, is an attempt at solving problems. Striving to make sense of strange mental experiences is only one example of the universal human desire to bring order to chaos." [12]

In the 1930s Brunton had a major influence in the West in the spreading of the knowledge of Eastern spirituality and his book *A Search in Secret India* inspired many to visit Ramana Maharshi. Among them was Alan Chadwick who became a stalwart in the ashram from the mid-1930s. Today, Brunton's books continue to inspire many on the spiritual path. If would indeed be ironic if this very same author had in some way helped dissuade Jung from seeing Ramana Maharshi.

A curious fact in respect to Brunton which has never been properly explained is the extensive use he made of Ramana Maharshi's teachings without specific acknowledgment. [13] We also have yet to read a comprehensive biography of Brunton. His son Kenneth Hurst did write a hagiography a few years after his demise but the facts were highly selective and raised more questions.

References

CHAPTER 1 The Avoidance of Pain and the Path Towards Happiness

1. https://www.mind.org.uk/information-support/types-of-mental-health-problems/mental-health-problems-introduction/causes/

CHAPTER 2 What a Therapist Offers

1. https://buddhiststories.wordpress.com/2012/11/03/kisa-gotami-and-the-mustard-seed/

2. https://www.karnacbooks.com/product/why-freud-was-wrong-sin-science-and-psychoanalysis/503/

3. Storr, A. *Feet of Clay. A Study of Gurus* (HarperCollins Publishers, 1996), p 91-97

4. https://www.booksfree.org/viktor-e-frankl-mans-search-for-meaning-pdf-free-download-a/

5. https://samaritansnyc.org/know-the-warning-signs/

6. https://en.wikipedia.org/wiki/Kintsugi

7. https://nobleharbor.com/tea/chado/WhatIsWabi-Sabi.htm

8. https://en.wikipedia.org/wiki/Mushin_(mental_state)

9. https://us.sagepub.com/en-us/nam/living-on-the-edge/book226528

10. Gordon-Brown, I. with Somers Barbara. *The Raincloud of Knowable Things*. (Archive Publishing, 2008)

11. Sharman-Burke, J. *The Complete Book of Tarot* (Pan Books 1995) p.25

12. https://en.wikipedia.org/wiki/Anaximander

13. https://www.labirintoermetico.com/09IChing/Wilhelm_R_The_I_Ching_or_Book_of_Changes_(abriged).pdf

14. Shpancer, N. When Talking Doesn't Cure: Negative Outcomes in Therapy. Psychology Today (March 2020

15. https://www.psychologytoday.com/us/blog/insight-therapy/202003/when-talking-doesnt-cure-negative-outcomes-in-therapy

16. https://www.emdr.com/what-is-emdr/

17. https://al-anon.org/al-anon-meetings/worldwide-al-anon-contacts/

18. https://www.aa.org/aa-around-the-world

19. https://workspublishing.com/

10. https://www.aa.org/alcoholics-anonymous-2014-membership-survey

21. https://eatingdisordersanonymous.org/

22. https://saa-recovery.org/our-program/the-twelve-steps/

23. https://www.gamblingtherapy.org/blog resource/gamblers-anonymous international directory world -wide-links/

24. https://virtual-na.org/meetings/

25. https://marijuana-anonymous.org/

CHAPTER 3 What Doctors Offer

1. World Health Organisation, Mental Disorders, September 2022.

2. https://www.nih.gov/news-events/news-releases/10-percent-us-adults-have-drug-use-disorder-some-point-their-lives

3. Panagioti, M Prevalence, severity, and nature of preventable patient harm across medical care settings: systematic review and meta-analysis BMJ 2019;366:l4185

4. Moncrieff, J., Cooper, R.E., Stockmann, T. et al. The serotonin theory of depression: a systematic umbrella review of the evidence. Mol Psychiatry (2022).

5. https://www.theguardian.com/society/2022/nov/05/study-finds-first-evidence-of-link-between-low-serotonin-levels-and-depression

6. https://bmjopen.bmj.com/content/bmjopen/7/4/e013384.full.pdf

7. https://www.england.nhs.uk/personalisedcare/social-prescribing/

8. Raguram, R., A. Venkateswaran, Jayashree Ramakrishna, and Mitchell Weiss.2002. Traditional Community Resources for Mental Health: a Report of Temple Healing from India BMJ 325, no. 7354: 38–40. doi:10.1136/bmj.325.7354.38.

9. Frueh BC, Knapp RG, Cusack KJ, Grunbugh AL, Sauvageot JA, Cousins VC, et al. Special section on seclusion and restraint: patients' reports of traumatic or harmful experiences within the psychiatric setting. Psychiatric Services 2005;56:1123-33

10. Fear, Neglect, Coercion, and Dehumanization: Is Inpatient Psychiatric Trauma Contributing to a Public Health Crisis?

CHAPTER 4 What a Guru Offers

1. Jung, C. G. *The Collected Works of C.G. Jung. Vol 11* (Princeton: Princeton: Princeton University Press 1969) p.577

2. https://archive.arunachala.org/newsletters/1998/jan-feb

3. Storr, A Feet of Clay - *A Study of Gurus* (Harper Collins, 1996) p 231.

4. Sri Ramanasramam, *Talks-With-Sri-Ramana Maharshi,* (Sri Ramansramam1994)

5. https://www.youtube.com/watch?v=FFyMG4mI_oQ

6. Sri Ramanasramam The Necklet of Nine Gems in *The Collected Works of Ramana Maharshi,* (Sri Ramanasramam 2001) p. 96

7. Osborne, A. *Ramana Maharshi and the Path of Self-Knowledge.* (Sri Ramanasramam 2002) p.7

8. Osborne, A. *The Teachings of Ramana Maharshi in His Own Words.* Preface, iii. (Sri Ramanasramam 2002)

9. https://en.wikipedia.org/wiki/I_Am_that_I_Am

10. https://selfdefinition.org/ramana/Talks-with-Sri-Ramana -Maharshi--complete.pdf p. 346

11. https://www.sriramanamaharshi.org/wp-content/ uploads/2012/12/who_am_I.pdf p. 34

CHAPTER 5 Choosing a Wounded Healer

1. https://watkinspublishing.com/books/carl-jung-wounded -healer-of-the-soul-by-claire-dunne/

2. Heron, John. in *Understanding the Placebo Effect in Complementary Medicine*. Peters. D. (Churchill Livingstone 2001)

3. https://www.youtube.com/watch?v=FFyMG4mI_oQ

4. https://link.springer.com/referencework entry/10.1007/978-0-387-71802-6_171

5. Sri Ramanasramam, *Talks With Sri Ramana Maharshi* (Sri Ramanasramam, 1994) p.170, Talk 198

CHAPTER 6 Inner Stillness versus Outer Intellect

[Chapter 6 first appeared as an article titled 'Cold Feet' in The Mountain Path. (2010) Vol 47 No. 3]

1. Brunton, P. *A Search in Secret India* (London: Rider & Co., 1934).

2. Zimmer, Heinrich. *Lehre und Leben des indischen Heiligen Ramana Maharshi taken from Tiruvannamalai der Weg zum Selbst* (The Way to the Self) (Zurich: Rascher, 1954)

3. Jung, C. G. *The Collected Works of C.G. Jung,* Vol 11 (Princeton: Princeton University Press 1969), p.576

4. Jung, C. G. *Memories, Dreams, Reflections* recorded and edited by Aniela Jaffe (New York: Vintage Books, 1989), p.23.

5. Brome, V. Jung: *Man and Myth* (London: Macmillan, 1978), p. 301.

6. Jung, C. G. *Memories, Dreams, Reflections* recorded and edited by Aniela Jaffe (New York: Vintage Books, 1989), p 56-57.

7. McGuire, W. *The Freud /Jung letters,* (Princeton: Princeton University Press, 1974), pp. 94-95

8. Jung, C. G. *Memories, Dreams, Reflections* recorded and edited by Aniela Jaffe (New York: Vintage Books, 1989), p 199.

9. Storr, A. *Feet of Clay. A Study of Gurus* (HarperCollins Publishers, 1996), p 91

10. Storr, A. *Feet of Clay. A Study of Gurus* (HarperCollins Publishers, 1996), p 96

11. Jung, C.G. *The Collected Works of C.G. Jung, Vol 11* (Princeton: Princeton University Press 1969), Para 958

12. Jung, C. G. *The Collected Works of C.G. Jung, Vol 11* (Princeton: Princeton University Press 1969), Para 957

13. Jung. C. G. *Memories, Dreams, Reflections* recorded and edited by Aniela Jaffe (New York: Vintage Books, 1989), p 305.

14. Storr, A. *Feet of Clay. A Study of Gurus* (HarperCollins Publishers, 1996), p 97

15. Zimmer, Heinrich. Lehre und Leben des indischen Heiligen Ramana Maharshi taken from Tiruvannamalai der Weg zum Selbst (The Way to the Self) (Zurich: Rascher, 1954)

16. Maharshi Ramana, *The Spiritual Teachings of Ramana Maharshi* (Boston: Shambhala, 1988).

17. Jung, C. G. *Letter to Countess Elizabeth Klinckowstroem L2, p.121 C.G Jung Letter Volume 2, selected and edited by Gerhard Adler in collaboration with Aneila Jaffe* (Bollingen Series: Princeton: Princeton University Press, 1953).

18. Hamlet Act III, scene II by William Shakespeare.

19. Dunne, C. *Carl Jung: Wounded Healer of the Soul. An Illustrated Biography* (Continuum, 2000), p203

20. Serrano, M. *Jung and Hermann Hesse: A record of two friendships* (Taylor Francis Books Limited), p.112

21. Jampolsky, G. *Love Is Letting Go of Fear,* (Celestial Arts 1982)

CHAPTER 7 The Doctor's, Therapist's and Guru's Happiness

[Chapter 7 first appeared as an article titled 'Knowing and Being' in The Mountain Path. (2023) Vol 60 No. 4]

1. Jung, C.G. *The Collected Works of C.G. Jung, Vol Eleven* (Princeton: Princeton University Press 1969), Para 957

2. Jung, C.G. *Letter to Countess Elizabeth Klinckowstroem L2, p.121 C.G Jung Letter Volume 2, selected and edited by Gerhard Adler in collaboration with Aneila Jaffe* (Bollingen Series: Princeton: Princeton University Press, 1953).

3. Jung, C.G. *The Collected Works of C.G. Jung, Vol Six* (Princeton: Princeton University Press 1969), para. 953

4. Face To Face Episode 8 BBC television series. Created and produced by Hugh Burnett October 22nd 1959

5. Jung, C.G. *Cryptomnesia. Coll. works, Vol., London:* (Routledge and Kegan Paul; United States Bollingen Foundation.1905)

6. Serrano, M. *Jung and Hermann Hesse: A record of two friendships* (Taylor Francis Books Limited), p.112

7. Maharshi, Ramana. *"Who am I?" Questions 23 & 24.* Sri Ramanasramam, 2008.

8. Sri Ramanasramam *Talks with Sri Ramana Maharshi* (Tiruvannamalai: Sri Ramanasramam, 1994, first published 1955), p 1-2.

CHAPTER 8 Mutual Aid Groups

[Chapter 8 is a shortened transcript of a talk given at Bristol's inaugural Al-Anon Convention on 31st January 2015. It was also the first chapter in Nimenko. Wasyl, The Spiritual Nature of Addictions, *(Goalpath Books, 2020)*

1. https://www.reddit.com/r/Jung/comments/cwpaqd/the_cofounder_of_alcoholics_anonymous_bill_ws/

2. https://silkworth.net/alcoholics-anonymous/dr-carl-jungs-letter-to-bill-w-jan-30-1961/

3. Nimenko, W. *The Spiritual Nature of Addictions,* (Goalpath Books, 2020) p. 9

CHAPTER 9 Spirit against Spirit

[Chapter 9 is a transcript from part of Chapter 9 in Nimenko. Wasyl, 'The Spiritual Nature of Addictions, *Goalpath Books (2020)]*

1. https://www.reddit.com/r/Jung/comments/cwpaqd/the_cofounder_of_alcoholics_anonymous_bill_ws/

2. https://silkworth.net/alcoholics-anonymous/dr-carl-jungs-letter-to-bill-w-jan-30-1961/

3. https://en.wikipedia.org/wiki/I_Am_that_I_Am

4. https://selfdefinition.org/ramana/Talks-with-Sri-Ramana-Maharshi--complete.pdf p. 346

CHAPTER 10 We are not born Unhappy

[Chapter 10 first appeared as an article titled 'The Way Out is In' in The Mountain Path. (2021) Vol 58 No. 2]

1. file:///C:/Users/Wasyl/Downloads/The-Story-of-a-Soul-Booktree.pdf p.4

2. Subbaramayya, G.V. *Sri Ramana Reminiscences* (Sri Ramanasramam. 1967) P 153

3. https://en.wikipedia.org/wiki/I_Am_that_I_Am

4. https://selfdefinition.org/ramana/Talks-with-Sri-Ramana-Maharshi--complete.pdf p. 346

5. Sri Ramanasramam *Talks with Sri Ramana Maharshi* (Tiruvannamalai: Sri Ramanasramam, 1994, first published 1955), p 322.

6. Sri Ramanasramam *Talks with Sri Ramana Maharshi* (Tiruvannamalai: Sri Ramanasramam, 1994, first published 1955), p 175.

CHAPTER 11 Pushed from Outside and Pulled from Inside

1. Osborne, A. *Ramana Maharshi and the Path of Self-Knowledge.* (Sri Ramanasramam, 2002)

2. Subbaramayya, G.V. *Sri Ramana Reminiscences* (Sri Ramanasramam. 1967) P 153

3. The Bible, *Psalm 46*

4. The Bible, *Luke 17:20-21*

CHAPTER 12 Experiential Knowledge

1. Muruganar, M. K. *Arunachala Akshara Mana Malai.*
Translated by Robert Butler. (Sri Ramanasramam, 2015)

APPENDIX

The Appendix is taken from Nimenko W. (2010) Cold feet. Part 11:- in 'The Mountain Path,' Vol 47 No. 3 2010.

1. Jung, C. G. *Letter from C.G. Jung to Gualthernus H. Mees,* Sept. 15, 1947. C.G. *Jung: Letters,* ed. Gerhard Adler (Princeton, 1973), Vol. I, p. 477.

2. Jung, C.G. *The Collected Works of C.G. Jung, Vol 11* (Princeton: Princeton University Press 1969) para. 952

3. Jung, C.G. *The Collected Works of C.G. Jung, Vol 11* (Princeton: Princeton University Press 1969), para. 953

4. Jung, C. G. *Letter from C.G. Jung to Gualthernus H. Mees,* Sept. 15, 1947. C.G. *Jung: Letters,* ed. Gerhard Adler (Princeton, 1973), Vol. I, p. 477.

5. Brunton, P. *A Search in Secret India* (London: Rider & Co., 1934).

6. Sri Ramanasramam *Talks with Sri Ramana Maharshi* (Tiruvannamalai: Sri Ramanasramam,1994, first published 1955), p204-205, para.250

7. Brunton, P. *The Hidden Teaching Beyond Yoga* (London: Rider & co., 1969, first published 1941), pp. 16-18.

8. Masson, J. *My Father's Guru: A Journey through Spirituality and Disillusion* (New York: Addison-Wesley, 1993), p.25

9. Storr, A. *Feet of Clay. A Study of Gurus* (HarperCollins Publishers, 1996), p. 163

10. Storr, A. *Feet of Clay. A Study of Gurus* (HarperCollins Publishers, 1996), p 165

11. Masson, J. *My Father's Guru: A Journey through Spirituality and Disillusion* (New York: Addison-Wesley, 1993), p.160

12. Storr, A. *Feet of Clay. A Study of Gurus* (HarperCollins Publishers, 1996), p 171

Notes on Chapters

CHAPTER 6 Doctor's and Therapist's Competition with Gurus

Chapter 6 first appeared as an article titled 'Cold Feet' in 'The Mountain Path.' Vol 47 No. 3 (2010)

CHAPTER 7 Thought, Stillness and Happiness

Chapter 7 first appeared as an article titled 'Knowing and Being' in 'The Mountain Path.' Vol 60 No. 4 (2023)

CHAPTER 8 Mutual Aid Groups

Chapter 8 is a shortened transcript of a talk given at Bristol's inaugural Al-Anon Convention on 31st January 2015. It was also the first chapter in Nimenko. Wasyl, The Spiritual Nature of Addictions, Goalpath Books, (2020)

CHAPTER 9 Spirit against Spirit

Chapter 9 is a transcript from part of Chapter 3 in Nimenko. Wasyl, The Spiritual Nature of Addictions, Goalpath Books (2020)

CHAPTER 10 We are not born Unhappy

Chapter 10 first appeared as an article titled 'The Way Out is In' in 'The Mountain Path.' Vol 58 No. 2 (2021)

APPENDIX

The Appendix is taken from Nimenko W. (2010) Cold feet. Part 11:- in 'The Mountain Path,' Vol 47 No. 3 (2010)

Bibliography

Brome, Vincent, *Jung: Man and Myth,* London: Macmillan, 1978.

Burnett, Hugh, *Face To Face Episode 8* BBC television series, October 22nd, 1959.

Brunton, Paul, *A Search in Secret India,* London: Rider & Co., 1934.

Brunton, Paul, *The Hidden Teaching Beyond Yoga,* London: Rider & co., 1969.

Dunne, Claire, *Carl Jung: Wounded Healer of the Soul. An Illustrated Biography,* Continuum, 2000.

Frankl, Victor, *Mans Search For Meaning,* Rider, 2004.

Gordon-Brown, I. with Somers Barbara, *The Raincloud of Knowable Things.* Archive Publishing, 2008.

Heron, John, in Understanding the Placebo Effect in *Complementary Medicine.* Peters. D. Churchill Livingstone 2001

Jampolsky, Gerald, *Love Is Letting Go of Fear,* Celestial Arts 1982

Jung, C. G., *The Collected Works of C.G. Jung.* Vol 11. Princeton: Princeton: Princeton University Press,1969.

Jung C.G., *Jung: Letters, Vol 1,* ed. Gerhard Adler, Princeton, 1973,.

Jung, C.G., *Jung: Letters Vol 2,* Selected and edited by Gerhard Adler in collaboration with Aneila Jaffe (Bollingen Series: Princeton: Princeton University Press, 1953.

Jung, C.G., *Memories, Dreams, Reflections* Recorded and edited by Aniela Jaffe, New York: Vintage Books, 1989.

Kropotkin, Peter, *Mutual Aid: A Factor of Evolution* - The Anarchist Library 1902

Masson, Jeffrey, *My Father's Guru: A Journey through Spirituality and Disillusion,* New York: Addison-Wesley, 1993.

Maharshi, Ramana, *The Spiritual Teachings of Ramana Maharshi,* Boston: Shambhala, 1988.

Maharshi, Ramana, *"Who am I?"* Sri Ramanasramam, 2008.

McGuire, William, *The Freud /Jung letters,* Princeton: Princeton University Press, 1974.

Moncrieff, J., Cooper, R.E., Stockmann, T. et al, *The serotonin theory of depression: a systematic umbrella review of the evidence.* Mol Psychiatry, 2022.

Muruganar, M. K., *Arunachala Akshara Mana Malai.* Translated by Robert Butler. Sri Ramanasramam, 2015

Nimenko, W., The Way Out is In. The Mountain Path. Vol 58 No. 2, 2021.

Nimenko, W., The Cuckoo Spirit in Searching for Wholeness in 'The Mountain Path.' Vol 48 No. 2, 2015.

Nimenko, W., Cold feet. Part 1 in 'The Mountain Path.' Vol 47 No. 2, 2010.

Nimenko, W., Cold feet. Part 2 in 'The Mountain Path.' Vol 47 No. 3, 2010.

Nimenko, W., Knowing and Being. The Mountain Path. Vol 60 No. 4, 2023.

Osborne, Arthur, *Ramana Maharshi and the Path of Self-Knowledge.* Sri Ramanasramam, 2002.

Osborne, Arthur, *The Teachings of Ramana Maharshi in His Own Words.* Preface, iii. Sri Ramanasramam, 2002.

Panagioti, Maria, *Prevalence, severity, and nature of preventable patient harm across medical care settings: systematic review and meta-analysis* BMJ ;366:l4185, 2019.

Peters, David, *Understanding the Placebo Effect in Complementary Medicine.* Churchill Livingstone, 2001.

Serrano, Miguel, *Jung and Hermann Hesse: A record of two friendships,* Schocken Books, 1971.

Shakespeare, William, *Hamlet Act III, scene II.*

Shakespeare, William, *Hamlet Act I, scene III.*

Sharman-Burke, Juliet, *The Complete Book of Tarot.* Pan Books, 1995.

Sri Ramanasramam, *Talks With Sri Ramana Maharshi*, 1994.

Sri Ramanasramam, *The Necklet of Nine Gems in The Collected Works of Ramana Maharshi*, 2001.

Storr, Anthony, *Feet of Clay - A Study of Gurus* Harper Collins, 1996.

Subbaramayya, G.V., *Sri Ramana Reminiscences* 1967. Sri Ramanasramam. P 108, 123

Thérèse de Lisieux,https://www.cmri.org/0-olmc-mission/catholic-books/storyofasoul.pdf

Webster, Richard, *Why Freud was Wrong*, Orwell Press, 1991.

Wilde McCormick, Elizabeth, *Living on the Edge: Breaking up to breakdown to breakthrough* Sage Publishing, 2003.

Wilehlm, Richard, *The I Ching or Book of Changes*, Routledge, 1968. Zimmer, Heinrich, *The Way to 'the self'* Zurich: Rascher, 1954.

Index

∞

∞

∞

∞

∞

∞

∞

∞

∞